GLASS
PAPERWEIGHTS

GLASS PAPERWEIGHTS
IN THE ART INSTITUTE OF CHICAGO

GERALDINE J. CASPER

THE ART INSTITUTE OF CHICAGO

Executive Director of Publications,
The Art Institute of Chicago: Susan F. Rossen
Edited by Peter Junker, Assistant Editor
Production by Katherine Houck Fredrickson

All photographs by
Christopher K. Gallagher, assisted by Chester Brummel,
Department of Imaging and Technical Services,
The Art Institute of Chicago, except:
pp. 6, 12 top, 59 by Carl Basner; pp. 9, 10, 11 by Robert Hashimoto;
p. 54 courtesy of Hunt Institute for Botanical Documentation, Carnegie Mellon University,
Pittsburgh, Pennsylvania;
p. 108 by Mort Kaye; rephotographed by Leslie Umberger

Art handling and organizational assistance
by Karen M. Johnson, Departmental Specialist,
European Decorative Arts and Sculpture, and Classical Art
Editing and production assisted by Elisabeth Dunn, David H. Krasnow, and Bryan Miller,
Department of Publications
Research assisted by Maureen Lasko, Senior Reference Librarian, and
Susan E. Perry, Senior Library Assistant,
Ryerson and Burnham Libraries, The Art Institute of Chicago
Photography coordinated by Paula Lee,
Department of Imaging and Technical Services

Designed by INFLUX CO., Chicago
Typeset in Berkeley by Paul Baker Typography, Inc., Evanston, Illinois
15,000 copies were printed on 157 gsm. U-Lite by
Dai Nippon Printing Co., Ltd., Tokyo

Objects illustrated in black-and-white on pp. 87, 88, 91 courtesy of
Lawrence H. Selman, L. H. Selman, Ltd.

The author wishes to thank Marjorie Cowan Geisler,
the librarians of Rakow Library, Corning Museum of Glass, Corning, New York, and of the
Neenah Public Library, Neenah, Wisconsin.
Special thanks to Jack W. Casper for his unfailing encouragement.

Front cover captions
Top: Compagnie des Cristalleries de Saint-Louis, concentric millefiori
with "dancing devils" silhouette in central cog cane,
signed *SL,* dated 1848 (p. 22, top).
Center: Compagnie des Cristalleries de Baccarat, coiled snake formed of
green filigree rod, c. 1848–55 (p. 19, bottom).
Bottom: L. J. Maës, Clichy-la-Garenne,
concentric millefiori pedestal, c. 1845–55 (p. 81).

Hardcover ISBN: 0–8109–3363–2 Softcover ISBN: 0–86559–091–5
Library of Congress Catalog Card Number:
90–086374

CONTENTS

THE CLASSIC PERIOD 7
Before Paperweights 9
The Debut 14
The Legacy 16
Baccarat 18
Clichy 20
Saint-Louis 23
American Variations 24

THOUSAND FLOWERS 27
Swirls, Crowns, and Marbries 35
Silhouettes 37

NATURE MAGNIFIED 45
Fauna 47
Silkworms 48
Pantin Lizard 49
Flora 53
Filigree 57
A Diverse Bouquet 65
Unknowns 66
Fruit 71

UNCOMMON INVENTIONS 75
Mushrooms and Pedestals 77
Specialties and Oddities 83
Overlays 87
Related Objects 92

TO REMEMBER 95
Cameos 98
Pinchbecks 102

COLLECTING 105

ARTHUR RUBLOFF, 1902–1983 108

CATALOGUE 109

GLOSSARY 118

SELECT BIBLIOGRAPHY 119

Elevation of the furnaces, and interior view of the Glass-house
and working operations.

Adapted from an illustration in Apsley Pellatt, Curiosities of Glassmaking (London, 1849), p. 65

THE
CLASSIC PERIOD

...the names Baccarat, Clichy,
and Saint-Louis are foremost...

The ideal glass paperweight, a sphere that might contain myriad mosaic patterns, webs of lacy filigree, a bounty of flora and fauna, or the image of an esteemed person, is a phenomenon of delight. A colorful, carefully arranged design, a moment of vision, is fixed forever under glass. It is difficult to imagine a better metaphor for the ideas of permanence and objectivity, and yet the very dome that captures this vision and invites our scrutiny also distorts and magnifies what we see, teasing our sight as the globe is turned and examined. If the dome is faceted or specially cut, the image can be seemingly shattered, multiplied, reduced, or animated with fleeting sparks of light. Part of the wonder of such an object might be the puzzle it presents: is it a kind of laboratory bell-jar, preserving some beautiful specimen of nature for analysis, or is it like a child's soap bubble, conjuring momentary flights of the imagination?

Glass paperweights were, beginning in 1845, a surprising commercial success during a time of economic depression in France and political uncertainty throughout Europe. Ostensibly made to hold down loose papers in drafty rooms, paperweights were actually more decorative than utilitarian. Perhaps this was part of what made them so appealing and generated a vogue that lasted until around 1855 in Europe and from around 1852 to 1888 in the United States. Paperweights were widely available in shops and stationers and displayed at many of the numerous international expositions of the last half of the nineteenth century. Today, an estimated thirty thousand of these so-called classic-period paperweights survive in collections throughout the world. As they periodically reappear in the marketplace, often with celebrated pedigrees, weights continue to set new auction records. To the uninitiated, it may be inconceivable that a palm-sized ball of glass can command such prices. But the attraction of paperweights is by no means limited to a small group of dedicated collectors. As donations of significant private collections are made to museums with increasing frequency — such as Arthur Rubloff's gift and bequest of 1,472 classic-period and contemporary weights to The Art Institute of Chicago — more and more people are able to experience the charms of these unusual and essentially intimate objects. Their inherent mystique, tantalizing and symbolic motifs, and apparent inviolability evoke wonder in the beholder. How were such intricate, tiny designs made from and encased in glass? Who had thought to make them, and what were the circumstances behind their diversity and popularity?

It is primarily the artistic influence and prodigious output of a few nineteenth-century French factories that we honor in calling the weights they produced "classic." The names of Baccarat, Clichy, and Saint-Louis are foremost on the list of glasshouses that consistently created exceptional weights, although other factories, in France, Venice, Bohemia, England, and the United States, produced notable examples and are also well represented in the Art Institute's collection. In fact, while many of the finest paperweights are clearly attributable to the three glasshouses named above, there are a number of examples — some worthy of being called masterpieces — for which we cannot identify a maker or, sometimes, a country.

Paperweights of the classic period were handmade by glassmakers who usually followed factory specifications for variables such as size, coloring, and pattern. Thus, similar weights of a given type, or sharing certain characteristics, often survive as evidence of a given factory's specialties. It is probable that unique paperweights were made to order or even as tests of the expertise and creativity of a young apprentice. Usually notable for exceptional artistry and color harmony, these unique examples represent the efforts of unremembered craftsmen in a medium with a long tradition of crediting only the factory. Authenticated weights that are "signed" or dated by the inclusion of slices of glass canes bearing the initials of the factory or the year are highly valued by collectors and literally priceless in documenting the history of the art. (Some fine examples of weights with signature or date canes follow, pp. 22, top; 31, top; 36, bottom).

The three major techniques used in making classic-period paperweights had existed for many years. One of these involved the manufacture of glass canes (called millefiori and filigree), and was familiar to the glassmakers of Antiquity; one (lampwork), also ancient, was originally a bead-making method that was refined during the Renaissance; and one (incrustation), while originating in the late eighteenth century, drew inspiration for its subjects from classical Greek and Roman art.

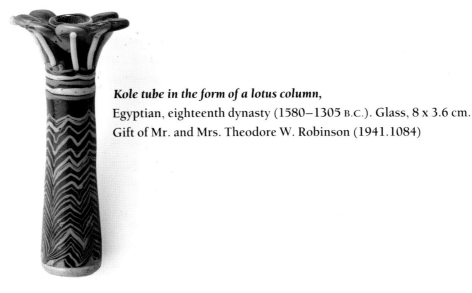

Kole tube in the form of a lotus column,
Egyptian, eighteenth dynasty (1580–1305 B.C.). Glass, 8 x 3.6 cm.
Gift of Mr. and Mrs. Theodore W. Robinson (1941.1084)

BEFORE PAPERWEIGHTS

It is not known who first made glass, but the oldest artifacts, colored beads from Mesopotamia and Egypt, date from around 3000 B.C. An Egyptian cosmetic tube in the collections (above), with a flared neck that mimics the sacred lotus flower, is a beautiful example of the core-form technique, one of the earliest methods for making glass vessels. In this process, a tubular, clay or straw plug was used as the core around which the basic shape of the container was fashioned of colored glass. The core was then broken and picked out, leaving the cavity. The exterior of this object was decorated by applying thin trails of hot white and yellow glass and "combing" them downward at intervals with a pointed tool. This method was adapted nearly two millennia later by the artists of Saint-Louis in making the festoon pattern of their marbrie weights (see p. 35).

The process from Antiquity with the greatest relevance to paperweight production was that of making canes. Canes are thin sticks of glass with either [a] embedded patterns running through them or [b] applied glass threads (usually white) running over them, lengthwise. The first variation is now called millefiori, the second, filigree. Canes are made by assembling rods of the desired colors and relative thickness, heating them until they fuse, and then pulling or drawing them out in a second heating. Drawing the cane miniaturizes its design. In the case of filigree, the cane is twisted while being drawn, producing a ropelike appearance as the threads coil around its surface, or, if the cane is made with threads coiling in

Network bowl,
Syrian, first century B.C.
Mosaic glass, 5 x 9.3 cm. Gift of Mr. and Mrs.
Theodore W. Robinson (1947.888)

different directions, producing a network effect. Canes were widely used in the Roman Empire to make vessels through the mosaic process, in which slices or segments of cane were arranged contiguously around a shaped core and fused. A network bowl (p. 10) illustrates the use of lengths of filigree canes, while a colorful fragment from a mosaic bowl (p. 11) displays the result of cross-cutting slices of millefiori canes to produce the repetition of a pattern. The artistic potential of this last mosaic technique reached its highest mark in the millefiori paperweights of the classic period.

The second major technique used in paperweights was lampwork, a way of modeling glass by manipulating it with tools over the flame of a lamp. Sharing in the spirit of curiosity and experimentation that characterized the Renaissance, glassmakers throughout Europe revived ancient methods and worked to perfect the decorative possibilities these allowed. An illustration in *Ars Vitraria Experimentalis* (1679 and 1689), a treatise on contemporary advances in glassmaking by the chemist Johann Kunckel (1630?–1703), shows three lampworkers seated around a table equipped with an elaborate bellows that could be pedaled to force air as needed to intensify the flames of their lamps (p. 12, top). Such state-of-the-art equipment was no doubt familiar to the artists of Nevers, France, who, by 1605, were making miniature figural sculptures using lampwork (see p. 12, bottom). It is recorded that, as a child, Louis XIII of France (1601–1643) played with "little glass dogs and other animals made at Nevers." Other *verre de Nevers* figures, often of mythological characters, saints, clergy, or nobles, sometimes include finely detailed depictions of expression, clothing, or hair. The mimetic facility of Nevers lampworkers was, however, greatly surpassed by their nineteenth-century counterparts, who created paperweights with incredibly realistic depictions of flora, insects, and animals. A sampling of *verre de Nevers* figures is displayed adjacent to the Arthur Rubloff Collection of paperweights at The Art Institute of Chicago.

The development of techniques for inserting cameo portraits (or other non-glass items) into glass coincided with Neoclassicism, the passionate eighteenth-century interest in ancient Greek and Roman art. One of the many aspects of classicism appropriated by Neoclassical artists was its emphasis on preserving the human likeness. Visitors to Italy eagerly purchased molded-glass copies of first-century Roman cameos, and, throughout Europe, artists and entrepreneurs — sometimes one and the same — strove to both imitate and emulate examples of this ancient vogue. The Scottish sculptor James Tassie (1735–1799) perfected a process for using glass paste to reproduce ancient carved gems. Tassie also provided patrons with their portraits in the form of finely detailed, miniature glass medallions. In 1769, Tassie was employed to supply molds of Greek mythological subjects to Josiah Wedgwood (1730–1795), whose pottery in Staffordshire, England, was perhaps the most successful at adapting classical motifs for the marketplace. One of Wedgwood's many popular ventures was a series of ceramic plaques, first offered in his 1773 catalogue, that depicts "The Heads of Illustrious Moderns from Chaucer to the Present Time." Contemporary subjects were not modeled from life, but taken from medals or wax reliefs. Such was the case with Wedgwood's medallion of the Swedish botanist Carolus Linnaeus (1707–1778), who is shown, just as the sculptor Carl Fredrik Inlander depicted him in a medal of 1774, with blooms of twinflower (*Linnea borealis*) in his buttonhole (p. 13).

It may have been in Bohemia that clay medallions were first incrusted in glass. The earliest patent for a cameo-incrustation process, however, was granted in 1818 to Frenchman Pierre Honoré Boudon de Saint-Amans, who had studied porcelain manufacture in England before returning to France around 1815 to work at Sèvres and other porcelain factories. In the collection of the Musée des Beaux-Arts in Agen, France, are two "paperweights" — not spherical, but shallow and plaquelike — with unidentified incrusted cameos by Saint-Amans, made between 1819 and 1829. In 1819, a patent was issued to Englishman Apsley Pellatt (1791–1863) for ornamental incrustations made from a paste of powdered glass and ceramic clay. Pellatt called this mixture "crystallo ceramie," but modern nomenclature now refers to such

Lampworkers,
illustration from Johann Kunckel, *Ars Vitraria Experimentalis*
(Frankfurt and Leipzig, 1689), fig. 10

Three* verre de Nevers *figures,
French, lampworked glass: boy with basket (left), late
eighteenth century, h. 8.3 cm; lady holding a garland
(center), c. 1775, h. 14.9 cm; girl in wide skirt, mid-
eighteenth century, h. 7.6 cm. Gifts of Mrs. Potter Palmer
through the Antiquarian Society (1941.1158,
1941.1150, 1944.1092)

compounds, as well as to the cameos and weights in which they are used, as sulphides. In Pellatt's process, the cameo, which could be painted with metallic colors, was encased in a blown "pocket of glass" that was afterward deflated and sealed. Such incrustations could then be applied to the surfaces of any number of glass objects. In 1821, Pellatt published *Memoir on the Origin, Progress and Improvement of Glass Manufactures,* which includes drawings of elegantly cut tableware, bottles, architectural elements, and desk accessories — including "press papers," the predecessors of spherical paperweights — each with incrusted sulphides. The subjects of these cameos are King George IV, the dukes of Wellington and de Berry, Shakespeare, Apollo, an Egyptian caryatid, the Muses, Venus, Julius Caesar, and Napoleon Bonaparte. Across the Atlantic, Pittsburgh glassmaker Benjamin Bakewell, quite likely inspired by an upcoming visit to the United States of the Marquis de Lafayette, produced a series of tumblers with cameos in their bases honoring the French hero. Similar Bakewell tumblers immortalize Andrew Jackson, DeWitt Clinton, Benjamin Franklin, and George Washington, each retailing for fifty cents in 1827.

Incrustation was not limited to cameos. Designs enameled on gold or silver foil were also incorporated as decorative elements in glass, especially during the years 1820–60. Such motifs were sometimes incrusted in lavishly cut or pressed tumblers by the glasshouses of Baccarat and Saint-Louis in France, Val Saint-Lambert in Belgium, and the Imperial Glass Factory in Saint Petersburg, Russia, among others. The broad acceptance of incrustation in a variety of glass items made it natural for these techniques to appear in paperweights of the classic period.

Medallion of Carolus Linnaeus
(Swedish, 1707–1778), English, early nineteenth century, Wedgwood pottery. Blue jasper with white jasper cameo-relief decoration, 10.5 x 7.6 cm. Gift of Mrs. Carl Christian Peters in memory of her husband (1954.144)

THE DEBUT

While the techniques for producing it were fairly well established by the 1830s, the glass paperweight as we now know it did not appear until diverse historical events forced glasshouses to seek new markets. The Napoleonic wars, which ended decisively with the peace imposed by the Congress of Vienna in 1815, had strained the economies of Europe. The sharply competitive milieu that followed, along with a declining market for luxury glass tablewares and chandeliers, seriously threatened the stability of prestigious French glasshouses such as Baccarat and Saint-Louis. It was a time for risk-taking and innovation. Bohemian glassmakers, after a long tradition of producing colorless wares, intensified efforts to dominate the market and introduced a broad new palette of gemlike, transparent colors. In Austria and Prussia, official associations for the encouragement of industry offered prizes for new scientific developments and incentives for establishing factories. And, as part of the spirit of progress that epitomized the age, trade fairs and expositions were organized in many of the major cities in Europe and the United States, stimulating technological and cultural competition as well as disseminating knowledge.

Pietro Bigaglia (1786–1878), a descendant of a centuries-old glassmaking family, produced at his several glasshouses on the Venetian island of Murano both finished wares and decorative components for a varied European market. As fashion shifted toward heavier, engraved glass from England and Bohemia, the demand for Bigaglia's fragile Venetian crystal dwindled. In 1826, to bolster his output, Bigaglia revived the process for making aventurine, by which thin copper-oxide particles are suspended in colorless glass. Bigaglia's aventurine expanded his European market and was even exported to America and China. The same year, Giovanni Battista Franchini (1804–1873), a lampworker who used a simple beadmaker's lamp fueled by animal fat, won the Venice Institute Award for glass imitations of pearls and coral to be used in jewelry. This accomplishment led to an alliance with Bigaglia, whom Franchini began to supply with thin lampwork rods for beads and, around 1840, with millefiori and filigree canes.

For the 1845 industrial exposition in Vienna, Bigaglia produced a set of small souvenirs that both showcased his wares and could be used as desk accessories. These essentially promotional trinkets were comprised of a layer of clear glass enclosing a randomly scrambled sampling of aventurine, filigree, and millefiori canes. They came in three forms: cubical, cylindrical, and spherical. Franchini supplied the souvenirs' commemorative *P B / 1845* canes, along with canes that portrayed in silhouette a dog, gondola, horse, pigeon, and rose. Tradition has it that the delegate of the Paris Chamber of Commerce, Eugène Péligot (1811–1890) of the Conservatoire des Arts et Métiers, immediately recognized that the spherical form of this somewhat unsophisticated souvenir was pregnant with profit potential for the depressed French glass industry. On his return to Paris, Péligot made an encouraging report to the Saint-Louis factory, which began to produce refined millefiori paperweights, as well as other desk accessories — pen vases, sealing-wafer trays, shot cups, and seals — some bearing the initials *SL* and dated that same year, 1845. By 1846, Baccarat was producing similar items.

The motifs of the earliest French weights, usually a closely packed arrangement of millefiori canes, appear just below the surface of the encasing glass, similar to Bigaglia's. Before long, however, a thicker gather of crystal came to be used for the dome, enhancing and magnifying the motif below and establishing the classic profile of the glass paperweight.

Market enthusiasm for paperweights in the French manner surpassed all expectations and generated intensive competition among leading French glasshouses. Throughout France and much of the Continent, curio cabinets and niches began to be filled with paperweights, which were even then recognized and collected as objects of art by discriminating collectors. All three glassmakers produced paperweights in three diameters: miniature, less than two inches; regular, two to three and one-fourth inches; and magnum, usually three and one-fourth to four and one-half inches. At first, all three factories solely used motifs of the versatile millefiori and filigree canes, creating an array of increasingly complex patterns.

Soon, however, the glasshouses asserted their identities by specializing in certain types, such as Saint-Louis's crown and marbrie weights (see pp. 34, top; 35); Clichy's swirls (see pp. 20; 34, bottom); or Baccarat's detailed sulphides, "Hunter and Dog" and Joan of Arc (see pp. 100–101, bottom). Individual elements also distinguished the three rivals. Baccarat and Saint-Louis each had their own repertory of figures appearing in silhouette canes. Clichy made such frequent and masterful use of the rose cane — a cane with imbricated staves made to resemble the overlapping petals of that flower — that, even though it was first introduced by Venetian glassmakers and used by many other factories, it became a virtual Clichy signature (see pp. 21, 26, 31). By 1848, millefiori patterns had begun to include lampworked blooms and bouquets, reflecting the current vogue for floral decoration and capitalizing on the popularity of sentimental "flower language." Lampwork techniques were used to create flowers that would not fade, just-picked fruits, exotic butterflies and insects, and perpetually coiled snakes. Sulphides of sacred or celebrated persons were augmented with vividly colored grounds or overlays, wreathed with millefiori canes, or, in the hands of master glass cutters, finished like fine gems.

THE LEGACY

Amilestone in nineteenth-century decorative arts was the Great Exhibition, held at the Crystal Palace, London, in 1851. That event, called the first world's fair, drew six million visitors and was attended almost daily by its sponsors, Queen Victoria and Prince Albert. Of the three major French factories, only Clichy exhibited paperweights at the Crystal Palace, although sulphides of the massive glass structure housing the event were produced in England by Allen and Moore and also in France (see p. 97, top). Two years later, Clichy exhibited again at the World's Fair in New York City. It appears that Baccarat and Saint-Louis conceded the then dwindling domestic paperweight market to their smaller rival and moved on to produce costly chandeliers and other luxury goods, which were again in demand in France by 1852, the outset of the Second Empire of Louis Napoleon.

There was a brief revival of interest in paperweights between 1870 and 1880. Some outstanding examples from that time have been conditionally credited to the Pantin factory, near Paris, sometimes referred to as "the fourth factory." Pantin did produce paperweights, but there is little documentation for the weights attributed to it (see p. 49). Between 1902 and 1925, attempts by Baccarat to revive the market failed, despite its offer to include the customer's choice of date for a modest fifty centimes extra (see p. 107). Although the paperweight production of French factories was never again to equal the years 1845–55 in terms of sheer volume, the influence of classic-style weights traveled to many other nations and their inspiration continues to be seen in glassmaking today.

In England, concentric millefiori "letter weights" by George Bacchus & Sons, Birmingham, were listed in the 1849 British Association Exhibition of Manufacturers and Art. Another Birmingham factory, Islington Glass Works, made millefiori weights that sometimes included the initials IGW and draft-horse silhouette canes, and the London glasshouse Whitefriars is thought to have made millefiori weights and inkwells, although this supposition lacks documentation. Overall, however, the number of paperweights made in England was very limited, perhaps less than four hundred by Bacchus and Islington combined. (Two Bacchus nosegays, or mushrooms, appear on pp. 76, 79.) Also small in number, but worthy of notice, are the weights from the Belgian glasshouse Val Saint-Lambert, near Liège. Unsigned examples from this great factory date from 1850 to 1900 (see p. 53).

Across the Atlantic, paperweights emerged, American style, from the glasshouses of Boston & Sandwich and the New England Glass Company in 1852. American interest in the form was probably encouraged by Clichy's exhibitions in London and New York. While the craze for classic, spherical paperweights had largely died out in America by 1880, their form lived on in the informal, folk-art objects made by glassworkers in their spare time, especially at two firms in the towns of Millville and Vineland, New Jersey. Paperweights with mottoes such as "Home

Sweet Home" and "Remember the Maine," or with the name of a loved one, were among the off-time creations variously known as frit, friggers, or off-hand glass. Around 1900, weights with floral motifs reappeared at Millville, displaying flowers with realistic petals made through the use of an innovative crimping tool (see p. 25, center).

It was the dedication and passion of a handful of twentieth-century collectors that led to the popular rediscovery of glass paperweights. Between 1935 and 1940, Evangeline Bergstrom of Neenah, Wisconsin, acquired more than three hundred classic-period paperweights and related glass items. Mrs. Bergstrom privately published the book *Old Glass Paperweights: Their Art, Construction, and Distinguishing Characteristics* in Chicago in 1940. The first comprehensive book dedicated to the subject, it was an immediate success and eventually inspired artists Charles Kaziun in the United States and Paul Ysart in Scotland to make millefiori and lampwork paperweights in the spirit of classic-period French examples. A full-scale paperweight renaissance began in 1952, when collector Paul Jokelson suggested that Baccarat and Saint-Louis revive the techniques of cameo incrustation to commemorate president-elect Dwight Eisenhower's inauguration and the coronation of Queen Elizabeth in 1953. Thereafter, until the 1980s, limited-edition weights by those historic glasshouses and by Cristalleries d' Albret immortalized contemporary figures of note.

In today's one- or two-person glassmaking environment, made possible through the revolutionary low-melting and long-working formula of chemist Dominick Labino (1910–1978), glass is a versatile medium for individual artistic expression. Along with Kaziun and Ysart, studio artists such as Paul Stankard and Debbie Tarsitano and numerous small, art-glass firms carry on the tradition of creating wonder in a ball of glass. It is a pleasure to illustrate in this volume some examples of the work of contemporary artists and workshops alongside the paperweights of the classic period that started it all.

BACCARAT

Founded in 1764, Compagnie des Cristalleries de Baccarat, in Alsace, gained renown for the lead-crystal wares it produced after 1824. In 1844, Baccarat began to make millefiori, filigree, and color-overlaid glass. When Saint-Louis introduced the first French paperweights, late in the following year, Baccarat followed suit, excelling in the precision and variety of its canes and patterns. Close millefiori, often set on a ground of upset white filigree to enhance the colors, was a specialty. Baccarat weights and desk accessories were enlivened by combinations of eighteen silhouette canes (see pp. 36–37). Garlands (see below and pp. 40–41) imitate formal French gardens, and carpet-ground weights evoke plantings of ground cover. In 1848, lampwork motifs appeared. Flowers, singly or in mixed bouquets, are usually set on colorless, sometimes star-cut grounds. Standardized petals and leaves were often used interchangeably to create flower variations. Baccarat had been a producer of cameo-incrusted drinking vessels since 1820, but spherical sulphide weights were not made until after 1846.

Sulphides were revived from 1953 through 1980; millefiori and lampwork types were revived in 1958 and 1970, respectively. Produced in limited editions, all contemporary weights bear Baccarat's twentieth-century logo: a line-drawn goblet, decanter, and tumbler, with the factory's name above and *France* below.

Garland-patterned millefiori, Baccarat, c. 1846–55 (cat. no. 11).
This masterful Baccarat paperweight includes a double trefoil garland of vibrant red and green canes, with bright yellow shamrock canes integrating the design. The entire arrangement is nestled upon a ground of lacelike, upset filigree. Although this paperweight bears no signature, the central arrow cane points to Baccarat as the maker.

Lampwork floral bouquet, Baccarat, c. 1848–55 (cat. no. 18).
This delicate, brightly colored bouquet captures the hues of a
summer garden and caters to Victorian sentimentality. The
pansy and rose symbolize true love, the primrose long life, and
the wheatflower prosperity. Encased in crystal, the carefully
crafted blossoms in lampwork paperweights are magnified and
illuminated by refracted light.

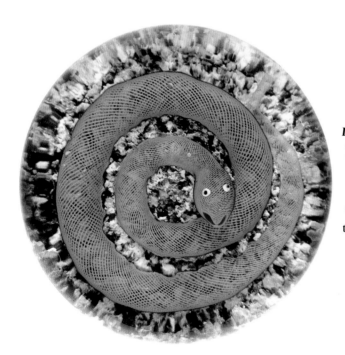

Lampwork snake, Baccarat, c. 1848–55 (cat. no. 25).
Pure fantasy, a Baccarat snake of gauzelike, spiraled green
filigree coils up and rests upon a sandy rock ground,
its eyes peering up at the viewer. Reptiles were relatively rare
among the animal motifs of the classic period, although
they were common symbols of renewal and youth.

CLICHY

The L. J. Maës factory, called Clichy because of its later location in Clichy-la-Garenne, was founded at Billancourt in 1837, by Rouyer and Maës, makers of glass novelties. About 1839, Maës and a new partner moved the business to Clichy, then a Paris suburb. By 1847, the firm's innovative paperweights and accessories were in demand, causing concern to the older houses of Baccarat and Saint-Louis. Millefiori weights, in over fifty different patterns and numerous color combinations, comprised about eighty percent of Clichy paperweight production. The palette ranges from conservative to spectacular, emphasizing combinations of pink, turquoise blue, purple, green, and garnet enhanced by white. Although few Clichy weights were signed, typical colors and patterns are distinctive to the trained eye. A "slumped" floret, or pastry-mold cane, often centers millefiori patterns. The rose cane made of flattened rods was practically a Clichy trademark, although research by Giovanni Sarpellon reveals that it derived from Venetian glass. Portrait sulphides of various notables were made, sometimes on brightly colored grounds (see pp. 98–99 top). Clichy's exuberant lampwork flowers — pansies, camellias, morning glories, clematis, and fanciful varieties of daisies and gardenias — have a refined, painterly quality that has long endeared them to collectors.

Tricolor swirl, Clichy, c. 1845–55 (cat. no. 34).
Contained within paperweight spheres, swirls seem to be captured in mid-spin, their momentum unspent. Colorful and dramatic, they have an energy and appeal quite different from those of delicate, millefiori gardens.

Lampwork bouquet, Clichy, c. 1848–55 (cat. no. 39).
A painterly daisy flanked by two morning glory
types (perhaps an experimental grouping) is set upon
Clichy's typically fine, white filigree ground. Of the
classic-period paperweight makers, only Clichy produced
the morning glory. Usually alone and sometimes
in clear glass, these delicate blossoms were created
in a variety of colors.

Patterned millefiori, Clichy, c. 1845–55 (cat. no. 35).
In this exceptional paperweight, a rich variety of Clichy
pastry-mold canes includes a pink rose and a rare
yellow rose. Although this type of rose cane, composed of
overlapping flat stave rods, was made earlier by
Venetians Dominic Bussolin and Giovanni Battista
Franchini, it was refined by Clichy. Almost a
trademark of the factory's glass paperweights, it became
known as the Clichy rose.

Concentric millefiori with two dancing devils, Saint-Louis, 1848 (cat. no. 66). Figural silhouettes, usually set within a cog cane, were added to the repertoire of Saint-Louis motifs in 1848 (see p. 39). This scarce example, signed and dated 1848, is exceptional for its large, central silhouette of two mischievous, dancing devils and its circle of camel, bird, dog, and dancing-figure canes.

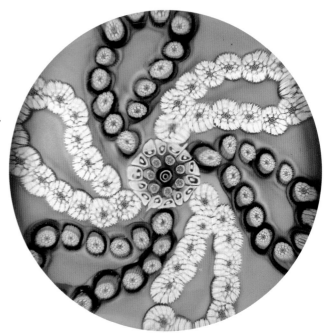

Patterned millefiori, Saint-Louis, c. 1846–55 (cat. no. 63). A vision of warmth and gaiety, this fanciful Saint-Louis millefiori loop pattern, rarely found on a salmon-orange ground, may be Saint-Louis's version of the popular Clichy swirl (see pp. 20; 34, bottom).

SAINT-LOUIS

Compagnie des Cristalleries de Saint-Louis was founded in 1586 and named in 1767 for the sainted King Louis IX (1215–1270). Late in 1845, it was the first firm in France to produce signed and dated millefiori paperweights and vases. Market control was soon challenged, however, by Baccarat and Clichy. Saint-Louis concentrated less on offering a wide variety of canes, colors, and patterns than its competitors, emphasizing instead close concentric arrangements and, by 1848, flat and upright lampwork floral motifs. Crown weights, with alternating ribbon twists and filigree, were a distinctive line (see p. 34, top). When Baccarat introduced silhouette canes, Saint-Louis did likewise (see p. 38). In lampwork, single flowers and flat sprays are among the most frequent motifs; the ubiquitous clematis and less common fuchsia, geranium, mum, and pompon usually appear on lattice-like, double-swirl grounds (see pp. 56–57 bottom), and dahlias on colorless grounds (see below). The sprightly colors and foliage of Saint-Louis's three-dimensional upright bouquets made them very popular. An upright bouquet is always contained in the factory's encased overlays (see p. 89); similar bouquets appear in exquisite filigree baskets with ribbon-twist handles (see p. 74). The factory's gilt, molded lizard on a hollow base (see p. 82) is one of the most dramatic deviations from the classic paperweight form. Although Saint-Louis paperweights were shown at the 1867 Paris Exposition, they were no longer regular production items, and were not revived for nearly a century.

Lampwork dahlia, Saint-Louis, c. 1848–55 (cat. no. 82).
A stylized dahlia, composed of five overlapping layers of star flowers, fills the entire sphere of this Saint-Louis paperweight. With its rare amber coloring and the clear contours of the overlapping petals, this weight conveys a remarkable sense of depth and texture.

AMERICAN VARIATIONS

Enthusiasm for glass paperweights in the United States can be traced to a hexagonal, plaque paperweight made by the New England Glass Company to honor Queen Victoria and Prince Albert, sponsors of the Great Exhibition. This souvenir, dated 1851, is the first evidence of American paperweight-making. Between 1852 and 1888, three Massachusetts glasshouses produced the majority of American weights: New England, Boston & Sandwich, and Mount Washington, all founded by glass technologist and entrepreneur Deming Jarves (1790–1869). Boston & Sandwich was the first American glasshouse to date scrambled millefiori weights, beginning in 1852.

New England Glass weights shown at the New York World's Fair in 1853 were reported by *New York Tribune* editor Horace Greeley to be "excellent examples of their class." If, at first glance, a New England nosegay or crown looks like a classic-period Saint-Louis weight, the resemblance was likely intentional. Not surprisingly, American weights generally exhibit the influence of immigrants trained in European factories. The stories of a few of these craftsmen are known to us. William Gillinder (1823–1871) trained in glassmaking in the Stourbridge area of England and learned millefiori techniques at George Bacchus & Sons before founding Gillinder & Sons in Philadelphia in 1867. François Pierre (1834–1872), renowned for the millefiori and blown-glass fruit weights he made at New England (see opposite, left), trained at Baccarat. Pierre may also have made New England's exceptional, magnum size, three-dimensional bouquets on double-swirl filigree grounds (see opposite, right).

Mount Washington, founded in 1837 in South Boston and moved to New Bedford in 1869, was a producer of tablewares and lamps, and a latecomer to paperweights. It undertook them through its expansion into art glass during the 1870s and 1880s. Mount Washington weights — undated, but sometimes documented — are spectacular examples of imagination and artistry. They were probably fashioned from special types of heat-sensitive glass that established the company's reputation as the "headquarters for art glass." Mount Washington's roses, often surrounded by butterflies (see p. 64), are the largest blooms in paperweights.

At the turn of the century, in Millville, New Jersey, American paperweight variations began to include roses made with a brass crimp to form the petals. Although lilies, roses, and tulips were created by a number of immigrant craftsmen using the same method in off-time at Whitall Tatum & Co., the best examples produced between 1900 and 1915 are credited to Ralph Barber (1869–1936). Barber, son of an English glassblower, is believed to have originated the crimp technique. His Millville roses (see opposite, center) have been widely copied. American glass paperweights, born in classic European traditions, have continued to evolve with an American accent. In the ongoing renaissance, new variations are still emerging.

Left: blown-glass apple, New England Glass Company, East Cambridge, Massachusetts, c. 1852–88 (cat. no. 94); center: footed rose with crimp-made petals, attributed to Ralph Barber, Millville, New Jersey, early twentieth century (cat. no. 117); right: faceted, three-dimensional bouquet on filigree ground, attributed to New England Glass Company, c. 1852–88 (cat. no. 97).

Patterned millefiori with five "C" scrolls, Clichy, c. 1845–55 (cat. no. 40).

THOUSAND FLOWERS

...the virtually boundless

decorative variety of millefiori...

Venetian glassmakers had, by the fifteenth century, rediscovered the Roman technique for making glass rods with designs extending end-to-end and drawing them into thin canes while they were hot and pliable. After the initial excavations of Pompeii in 1755, European interest in ancient glass intensified. In *Recollections of Antiquity* (1756), the Comte de Caylus detailed mosaic-glass methods with great accuracy and reported a thriving market for small antiquities and copies of ancient glass. The first to capitalize on this new trend were the glassmakers of Venice.

While segments of cane were used in different processes to make Roman-inspired bowls or other objects, it was the so-called Venetian ball, a globe-shaped, pell-mell arrangement of varicolored canes encased in clear glass, that held the potential for the virtually boundless decorative variety of millefiori paperweights. An ancient Venetian ball was illustrated in Apsley Pellatt's *Curiosities of Glassmaking* (1849), indicating its status among mid-nineteenth-century glassmakers as an item worthy of investigation. Curiosity expressed in 1495 by the librarian Marcantonio Sabellico (and often quoted since) was elicited by the Venetian ball, but also anticipated the marvel that classic-period paperweights would inspire: "To whom did it first occur to include in a little ball all the sorts of flowers that clothe the meadows in spring?" Some of the poetry of Sabellico's statement is shared by the term millefiori — literally, "thousand flowers" in Italian — which was coined in the eighteenth century and is now used to describe the canes as well as the objects they decorate.

Brought to near perfection by French glassmakers, the millefiori concept paralleled the concurrent vogue in Victorian England for horticulture and flower language — the expression of personal sentiment through gifts or images of symbolic blooms. Floral imagery was effectively exploited in the weight shown opposite. An arrangement of Clichy's flared, pastry-mold canes projects the vision of a carefully landscaped garden with edelweiss, rose, and other blooms forming the factory's initial. The large center cane is reminiscent of a garden sculpture or fountain, and the grasslike ground studded with tiny white starflowers evokes the verdancy of spring.

Pietro Bigaglia's informal assembly of rods, silhouettes, sparkling bits of aventurine, and signature and date canes (see below) echoed the Renaissance Venetian ball while looking forward to many of the elements of classic-period paperweights. Like Bigaglia's prototypes, some of Saint-Louis's early, close millefiori weights (see opposite, top) were initialed and dated, but did not make use of the magnifying nature of the dome. Factories in Bohemia, England, and the United States joined the French in borrowing from Bigaglia's weights. Bigaglia's "Catherine's wheel" rods were translated into swirl patterns; florets were varied in countless close and patterned millefiori motifs; filigree and ribbon twists were used to form crown weights, grounds, and torsades. The torsade that coils around the perimeter of a weight of unknown origin (opposite, bottom) is a refinement of a Bigaglia colored rod within spiraled filigree. Even Bigaglia's haphazard gather of cane pieces was copied, as a number of so-called scrambled weights were produced by Saint-Louis, Clichy, Boston & Sandwich, and New England Glass Company. Formally uncomplicated, scrambled weights still maintain their charm — intriguing the viewer just as their Bigaglia precursors did in May 1845.

Like Bigaglia's ideas, Clichy's inventiveness was not easily ignored. Many different patterns and effects were achieved with basic six-point-star, whorl, pastry-mold, and rose canes, all closely packed. Although rarely signed with a *C* (see p. 31,

Scrambled millefiori, Pietro Bigaglia, 1845 (cat. no. 98).
The Venetian glassmaker Bigaglia exhibited the first signed and dated millefiori paperweights in Vienna at the Exhibition of Austrian Industry in May 1845. His souvenir paperweights, with their scrambled millefiori, silhouette, and wheel canes, filigree twists, and bits of aventurine, display design elements that were later adapted to French, Bohemian, and American paperweights.

Close millefiori, Saint-Louis, c. 1845–46 (cat no. 87).
The magnifying potential of the glass paperweight dome has not
been fully exploited in this early Saint-Louis example.
However, the somewhat haphazard arrangement of canes seen
in Bigaglia's scrambled millefiori weight (opposite) has
been refined and disciplined.

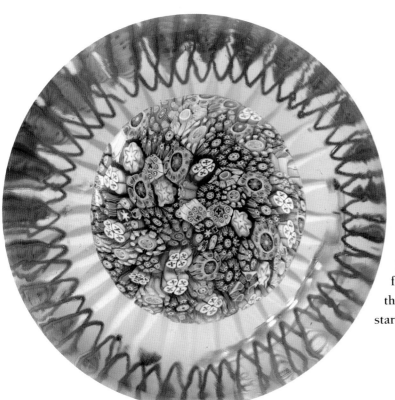

***Close millefiori mushroom, origin unknown, possibly
French or Bohemian, c. 1846–55 (cat. no. 102).***
When viewed from the side, this weight reveals canes
drawn into a narrowing cluster, like the stems
in a bouquet, or the stalk of a mushroom. Although closely
packed millefiori canes are the most common form
for Baccarat mushrooms, this example, unusual for
the predominance of blue, salmon, and green
star and cog canes, includes an uncharacteristic torsade.

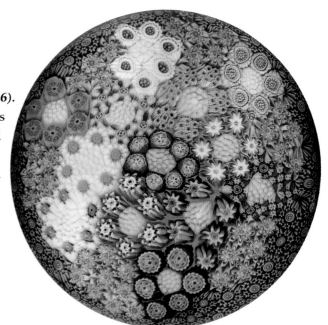

Patterned millefiori, Clichy, c. 1845–55 (cat. no. 36). In this rare Clichy paperweight, closely packed millefiori canes are grouped in bursts of color, in a deceptively casual arrangement. The overall effect is of a miniature meadow with wildflowers in full bloom.

top), Clichy weights often include the stave-rose cane. Thirty-two Clichy roses appear in the square arrangement illustrated opposite (bottom); as many as sixty-six such roses are known in a unique example. Clichy's precise workmanship and subtle variations of warm colors suggest gardens at their peak. On grounds that are clear, colored, or composed of lacy filigree or grasslike "moss" canes, these arrangements evoke in miniature the ordered landscapes of Versailles as well as imaginative, bird's-eye views of flowering French fields. In one example (p. 32, top), a Bohemian competitor may have imitated not only the Clichy rose and edelweiss canes but also the stave basket that contains a mushroom-shaped bouquet. A Clichy specialty, called a checker, used barber-pole ribbon twists of white filigree segments to frame spaced millefiori florets. A checker with three pastel colors of filigree (p. 32, bottom) is extremely unusual. A competitive version by Saint-Louis of Clichy's six-point-star pastry-mold cane can be seen in a concentric millefiori on a striking, yellow ground (p. 33, top). Saint-Louis garland patterns (also rare) appear on intensely colored opaque grounds. Typical Saint-Louis six-point-star canes can be seen arranged in a garland pattern that, appropriately, forms a six-point star (p. 33, bottom). All of these variations, creatively making use of basic millefiori elements and techniques, are treasures to be sought and preserved.

Carpet ground with florets, Clichy, c. 1845–55 (cat. no. 42).
Small millefiori florets, like early springtime blossoms emerging
through a light blanket of snow, decorate this very rare, white
stardust-cane carpet ground. A special feature of this weight is
its signature cane, bearing the initial *C*.

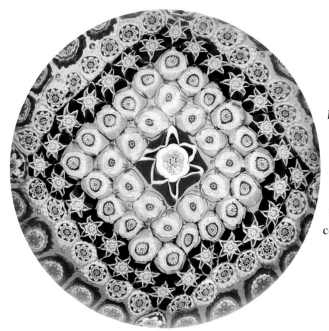

Patterned millefiori with square design, Clichy, c. 1845–55
(cat. no. 37). This Clichy paperweight may be unique.
Its square design recalls the carefully patterned flowerbeds of
formal French gardens. Two rows of Clichy roses, in
shades of pink and green, appear among other florets in concentric squares around the large red, white, and blue
center cane.

Patterned millefiori, origin unknown, probably Bohemian, c. 1845–55 (cat. no. 101). Formerly attributed to Clichy, this loosely arranged basket of roses has a more casual air than many millefiori compositions. A blue-and-white basket holds large Clichy-type roses that appear to be of Bohemian origin.

Checker, Clichy, c. 1845–55 (cat. no. 41). Paperweights with millefiori and pastry-mold canes framed in a checker arrangement were a Clichy specialty. The use here of a variety of colors (pink, pastel green, pastel blue, and white) for the filigree cane segments is unusual, perhaps an experiment to create a novel effect.

Concentric millefiori, Saint-Louis, c. 1845–55 (cat. no. 58).
This Saint-Louis motif of seven alternating circles of blue-and-white and red-and-white star canes on a chartreuse-yellow ground is one of only two known examples.

Star-patterned millefiori garland, Saint-Louis, c. 1845–55 (cat. no. 59). Since Saint-Louis garland paperweights seldom include a colored ground, this is an unusual piece. The deep royal-blue ground accents the delicate millefiori canes.

Crown, Saint-Louis, c. 1845–55 (cat. no. 60).
The crown paperweight, an adaptation of sixteenth-century
Venetian techniques for filigree-decorated goblets, bowls, and
vases, was a Saint-Louis specialty. Unlike most classic
glass paperweights, it is hollow, made by blowing colorless
glass into a mold lined with twisted rod elements.

Swirl, Clichy, c. 1845–55 (cat. no. 45).
Although the two-color swirl in this paperweight is a common
Clichy motif, the cross of millefiori canes is an unusual variation.
Clichy's swirl design is usually centered by a
single pastry-mold cane or, occasionally, a rose (see p. 20).

Marbrie, Saint-Louis, c. 1846–55 (cat. no. 61).
The hollow marbrie, another Saint-Louis specialty, is rare when
festooned with more than one color on white. The swag
design is made by trailing colored glass threads around a sphere
of white glass and pulling them up or down at intervals.

SWIRLS, CROWNS,
AND MARBRIES

As millefiori motifs became more sophisticated and diverse, some variations became almost synonymous with certain factories. Such was the case with the Clichy swirl, an adaptation of Venetian filigree that suggests the playful optics of a toy pinwheel, but with antecedents in ancient symbols for eternity and in the medieval sign of Saint Catherine's wheel. Although a version of the swirl was made in Bohemia, Clichy's exemplifies French paperweight expertise.

At Saint-Louis, competition from Clichy probably motivated the development of its distinctive crown and marbrie weights. Unlike most classic weights, crowns and marbries are blown, and, therefore, hollow. Crowns encase alternating white filigree with colored ribbon twists. To make them, canes are arranged vertically in a cup-shaped mold, into which clear glass is blown. They are capped by a floret or, occasionally, a silhouette cane. Inspiration for marbrie weights was derived from ancient vessels and the combing technique that was used to effect a festooned decoration. The marbrie (a derivation of *marbre*, French for marble) is a sphere overlaid with opaque white glass and trailed horizontally with colored threads, which are pulled while hot to form looped quadrants. Marbries are usually centered by a single floret, but sometimes by a cluster of canes. An extraordinary and rare variation of the marbrie is crowned by a gilt, coiled lizard of molded glass (see p. 82).

Carpet ground with arrow, geometric, and silhouette canes, Baccarat, 1848 (cat. no. 16). This effective Baccarat variation offers a generous sampling of arrow canes and Gridel animal silhouettes, highlighted by their placement on a flower-like carpet ground of white-and-blue cog canes.

Spaced millefiori with silhouette canes, Baccarat, 1847 (cat. no. 14). A full four inches in diameter, this Baccarat paperweight is a veritable zoo of animal silhouette canes: of the fourteen silhouettes, the dog, rooster, and elephant each appear twice. Among the other animals featured are a monkey, a dove, a horse, and a squirrel. The ground of white filigree and yellow-and-pink ribbon-twist segments creates a festive mood.

SILHOUETTES

In the hands of Baccarat designers and craftsmen, millefiori colors and patterns were greatly refined and diversified. A typical close-millefiori paperweight used from 150 to 200 canes, a variety that took weeks to create. Between 1846 and 1847, eighteen animal and figural silhouettes began to add yet another element to the factory's production. Somewhat reminiscent of Giovanni Battista Franchini's silhouettes that appeared in Bigaglia's souvenir paperweights beginning in 1845, Baccarat's charming images at once expanded the factory's horizons and almost endlessly varied its millefiori arrangements.

Though silhouettes were a widely popular form of portraiture, in paper cut-outs as well as on ceramics and glass, Baccarat's silhouettes derived from child's play. The general manager of the factory discovered a number of white-on-black paper cut-outs of animals made by his nine-year-old nephew, Joseph Emile Gridel, during a visit to the boy's family. Shortly after the manager's return, Baccarat introduced its selection of eighteen figures: bird, butterfly, deer, devil, dog, elephant, goat, horse, hunter, a pair of lovebirds, monkeys in black and white, pelican, pheasant, rooster, squirrel, stork, and swan. These were used in various combinations, no more than twelve different subjects to a weight.

Silhouettes appear in Baccarat close and patterned paperweights, and highlight

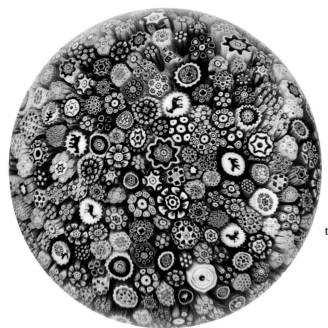

Close millefiori, Baccarat, 1848 (cat. no. 15).
A magnificent example of Baccarat versatility and precision, this glass paperweight incorporates a vast array of millefiori canes and colors. Arrow, trefoil, shamrock, flower, and a rich variety of silhouette canes cover the ground in the true spirit of the "thousand flowers" ideal.

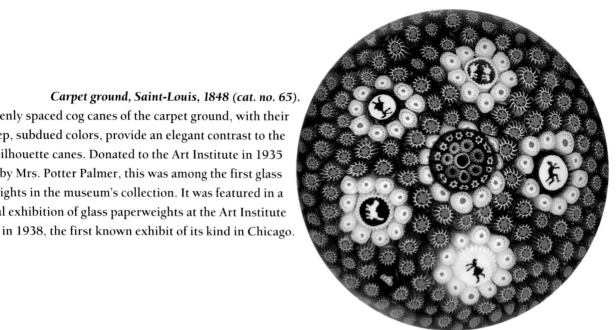

Carpet ground, Saint-Louis, 1848 (cat. no. 65).
Here, the evenly spaced cog canes of the carpet ground, with their deep, subdued colors, provide an elegant contrast to the intricate silhouette canes. Donated to the Art Institute in 1935 by Mrs. Potter Palmer, this was among the first glass paperweights in the museum's collection. It was featured in a special exhibition of glass paperweights at the Art Institute in 1938, the first known exhibit of its kind in Chicago.

Paneled jasper, Saint-Louis, c. 1848 (cat. no. 68).
Jasper, a mixture of tiny, colored glass chips rolled into a gather of hot glass, was a Saint-Louis specialty. This type of paneled jasper motif was a variant that was usually used to dramatize a silhouette cane (a dancing lady, in this example). Occasionally, a fine, blue-and-white miniature swirl tops the motif.

garland arrangements, but are seldom seen in mushrooms or double overlays. Spaced millefiori motifs with silhouettes were occasionally dated during the years 1847 through 1849, the latter being rare and without the signature B. *B/1848* is the only date used in Baccarat carpet grounds. Although most silhouettes are white on black ground, within a colored cog cane, they may be red, dark blue, mauve, black on white, or white on blue or green. It is interesting to compare the silhouettes in the illustrated examples. The multiplicity of Baccarat millefiori paperweights promises that there will always be another combination to discover.

Saint-Louis's silhouettes, like those of Baccarat, were effective schematic elements used to highlight close concentric, spaced, and carpet-ground millefiori arrangements. Counterparts to Franchini's prototypes, with their symbols of Venetian life, the silhouette canes of Saint-Louis seem to tell of a carefree French bourgeoisie. A dancing couple, dancing lady, and dancing man, along with the mischievous running devil and pair of dancing devils, are accompanied by an unlikely menagerie comprised of an anteater, camel, dog, horse, and turkey. Two varieties of flowers complete the set of twelve silhouettes.

Saint-Louis silhouettes, usually black on white in a typical Saint-Louis cog cane, are bonuses most commonly found in scrambled and concentric examples. Although silhouettes only occasionally appear in them, Saint-Louis carpet grounds sometimes contain five large silhouette canes spaced around a central floret, as in the example illustrated opposite, at top. Similar concentrics, when centered by a large silhouette, may include a circle of various different silhouettes or, more rarely, a circle of canes repeating a smaller image of the same figure. Such examples have the enchanting appeal of folk art.

The panel arrangement on a mottled ground known as jasper (see opposite, bottom) may be Saint-Louis's version of the Clichy swirl. A kind of fanciful wheel with spokes that resemble trails of thick cake frosting secured by moundlike florets, this paperweight gives the impression of having emerged from some fairy-tale cottage. Its most endearing feature is no doubt the lively dancing-lady silhouette at its center. There is also a surprise near the base of this example, where a blue-and-white torsade, invisible from the top, circles the sphere.

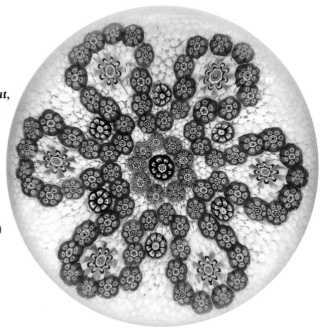

Garland-patterned millefiori on carpet ground, Baccarat, c. 1846–55 (cat. no. 10). The meandering pattern of this paperweight's six-loop millefiori garland, set upon a white, stardust-cane carpet ground, gives it a festive air. This rare Baccarat paperweight was compared by Paul Hollister to a "formal garden whose flowers are set in a ground of white pebbles." (*Encyclopedia of Glass Paperweights* [New York, 1969], p. 56)

Garland-patterned millefiori, Clichy, c. 1848–55 (cat. no. 50). A superb double quatrefoil Clichy garland, including edelweiss and rose canes, rests on a grasslike ground highlighted by tiny white stars. Although garland patterns were made by Baccarat and Saint-Louis, the vast majority were made by Clichy, which produced them on a variety of carpet grounds. Here, the deep green provides a lush background.

***Garland-patterned millefiori with silhouettes,
Baccarat, c. 1848–55 (cat. no. 21).*** In this rare, complex,
cinquefoil garland, each loop, centered by a large
animal silhouette cane, is composed of a different type of
floret. Shamrock canes are unusual in a garland, as is
the upset filigree ground. The central arrow cane, however,
is almost a Baccarat trademark. Baccarat garlands,
usually double trefoil or circlet, are among
the factory's loveliest motifs.

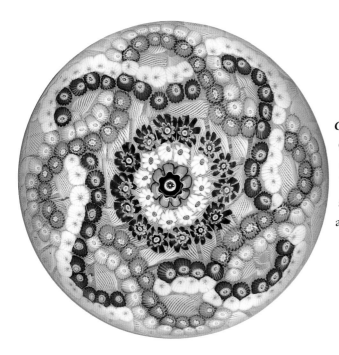

Garland-patterned millefiori, Clichy, c. 1845–55 (cat. no. 44).
Clichy's glass gardeners outdid themselves in this
complex garland of intertwined quatrefoils set on a froth of
lacy filigree. Four quatrefoils of millefiori canes
are intricately woven together, creating a sense of depth
and three-dimensionality.

Flat lampwork bouquet with garland, Saint-Louis, c. 1848–55 (cat. no. 83). In 1848, the revival of lampwork techniques in paperweights enhanced and multiplied Saint-Louis motifs significantly. Here, lampwork leaves, added to millefiori florets, compose a beautiful nosegay and garland.

Patterned millefiori, New England Glass Company, c. 1852–88 (cat. no. 93). This paperweight shows a Saint-Louis influence in its millefiori cane designs and the spoke pattern on a double-swirl filigree ground. Bohemian-style quatrefoil faceting and three narrow flute cuts between each lobe create the illusion of a nosegay motif when viewed from above.

***Millefiori and lampwork sprigs, Saint-Louis, c. 1848–55
(cat. no. 78).*** A variation of the Saint-Louis nosegay motif
(opposite), these single sprigs (millefiori florets with
lampwork leaf and stem) appear to be casually tossed onto
a ruby pool. This rare arrangement, made only by
Saint-Louis, is also known to have been made on a colorless
ground, and sometimes faceted.

"Mistletoe," Francis Dyer Whittemore, c. 1960s–'70s (cat. no. 123).
Francis Dyer Whittemore was one of the first contemporary artists
to make paperweights entirely by lampwork. His single
flowers, crimp roses, and Christmas motifs — like this sprig of
mistletoe on a translucent cobalt-blue ground — are well
known. Whittemore's use of millefiori slices is a subtle echo
of the Saint-Louis sprigs (above) and bouquet with
garland (opposite, top).

Profile of "Silkworms," lampwork paperweight, possibly Pantin factory, c. 1878 (p. 48, cat. no. 57)

NATURE
MAGNIFIED

...garden varieties and

exotic species...

In 1760, the French encyclopedist Denis Diderot wrote: "There is no object that cannot be made with [glass] enamels worked in the heat of the lamp in only a few moments...depending on one's proficiency in the art of modeling." The lampworking process, in which glass is shaped or fused from rods melted over the flame of a lamp, probably descended from Bronze Age metalsmithing procedures. During the Renaissance, extensive lampwork glass tableaux ornamented French and Italian rooms. These included animals, gardens, and figural scenes from mythological, religious, or secular tales. Although early clay lamps were followed by metal types with more efficient wicks, the process was essentially unchanged until the adoption of the Bunsen burner at the end of the nineteenth century. The lampwork motifs in paperweights of the classic period not only indicate their makers' technical proficiency, but also, in the subjects they depict, mirror their time's fascination with the natural world.

The exploration of Asia, the Near East, and the Americas by trading companies in the sixteenth and seventeenth centuries fostered the planting of exotic gardens and the collecting of natural oddities. In France, collections of curios were amassed by naturalists such as Bernard Palissy (1510–1590). It was typical of these personal museums to include shells, teeth, feathers, and petrified insects alongside carvings, clothing, weapons, and other novelties from foreign cultures. Palissy, also a ceramist whose wares are known for their decoration of realistic fish, insects, and mollusks, was a forerunner of the artists who modeled creatures in glass for paperweights. His ceramics inspired imitators working in the neo-Renaissance style of the mid-nineteenth century, when decorative artists were reexamining older styles through a succession of revivals. Palissy-revival platters could well have been offered by the same purveyors who sold lampwork paperweights, the newest and most purely decorative manifestation of the naturalist's quest for curios.

Lampwork pompon with butterfly, Baccarat, c. 1848–55 (cat. no. 24). Made almost exclusively by Baccarat, lampwork butterflies are placed above floral motifs encased in clear glass to create the illusion of their hovering in space. In this example, slices of millefiori canes, lined with white, form the wings; the body is fashioned from fine amethyst filigree rod. Baccarat butterflies most often appear above a white clematis and occasionally are found with a wheatflower, pansy, or primrose; but they seldom appear above a white pompon, as here.

Lampwork butterfly with flowers, possibly Saint-Louis, c. 1848–55 (cat. no. 90). Butterfly motifs by Saint-Louis are extremely rare and usually appear on double-swirl white filigree ground. In this example, the millefiori-cane wings and body, as well as the flowers, may be unique, perhaps an attempt to outdo Baccarat's profile butterfly (opposite).

FAUNA

The delightful naiveté of the earliest lampwork fauna is too often qualified as the immature work of yet inexpert factory craftsmen. Because many later paperweights, such as the celebrated "Silkworms" (pp. 44, 48), exhibit both great technical merit and a high degree of naturalism, it is presumed that a refinement of technique occurred that allowed for increasingly realistic depictions. It could also be true, however, that this evolution, from general observation to exact taxonomy, was a predictable reflection of a change in how people considered and interpreted nature. As the century progressed, the realm of nature seemed ever more scientific than symbolic.

While their images became more lifelike, the creatures selected for imitation nonetheless retained their traditional significance. Snakes and lizards, while not possessing the qualities of conventional beauty, relate to ideas of rebirth and renewal. Just as the butterfly emerges from a deathlike, pupal state, so reptiles shed their old skins for apparently youthful ones.

Contemporary lampwork fauna runs the gamut of zoological and stylistic types, stressing both the beauty of the creature and the individuality of the craftsman.

Lampwork butterfly with flowers, Baccarat, c. 1848–55 (cat. no. 17). This Baccarat butterfly appears in profile, with millefiori wings raised and six amethyst legs resting lightly on the stem of purple bellflowers. This delightful lampwork flight of fancy, made prismatic by concave facets (printies) on the top and side, suggests a momentary glimpse of a sunlit garden.

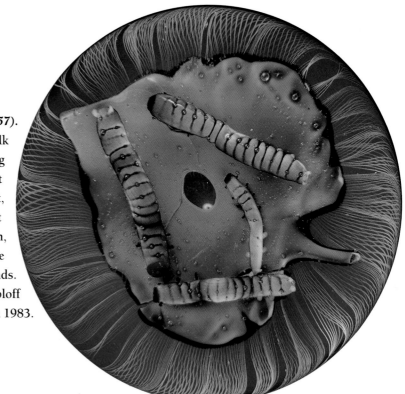

"Silkworms," possibly Pantin, 1878 (cat. no. 57).
The use of radiating filigree to suggest the weaving of silk strands is a masterful conception. Another fascinating aspect of "Silkworms" is its provenance. In the 1920s, it entered the collection of Mrs. Applewhaite-Abbot, which was sold at auction in 1953. King Farouk of Egypt instructed a dealer to purchase it for his collection, but was forced to abdicate his throne the very day of the auction, leaving the weight in the dealer's hands. Paul Jokelson was its next owner, from whom Arthur Rubloff acquired it at auction in 1983.

SILKWORMS

No other object in the Art Institute's paperweight holdings has captured the imagination of connoisseurs and visitors to the Arthur Rubloff Collection as the "Silkworms" paperweight has. Speculation about the origin and subject of this unsigned and undocumented weight has added to its attraction over the years.

In 1948, Roger Imbert and Yolande Amic, in the book *Les Presse-papiers français*, suggested that it may have been specially made by Saint-Louis in 1848 for a Lyons silk manufacturer. However, when the weight is examined under a long-wave ultraviolet lamp — an inexact but helpful method of comparing weights by observing differences in fluorescence caused by the chemical composition of their glass — the crystal of "Silkworms" differs markedly from that of signed Saint-Louis examples. While Saint-Louis crystal regularly (but not always) fluoresces a cloudy coral-pink, "Silkworms" reflects a grayish blue-green similar to the fluorescence of eleven lizard weights attributed to Pantin (see opposite).

Another explanation may be more plausible: Pantin may have made this weight for the Paris Exposition Universelle of 1878 to commemorate the work of microbiologist Louis Pasteur (1822–1895), who spent three years investigating a disease that was decimating the silkworm stock in the south of France. Pasteur's efforts led to a method for preventing the disease and saved the French silk industry from certain ruin.

PANTIN LIZARD

Little is known about Cristalleries de Pantin, even though it is credited with some of the most exquisite lampwork paperweights of the nineteenth century. Reconstructing the puzzle of Pantin begins with an account by Charles Colné, U.S. Commissioner to the 1878 Paris Exposition. In Colné's official report, he mentioned the exhibition by Pantin of "paperweights of solid glass...containing glass snakes, lizards...millefiori of roses, leaves and fruit." Unfortunately, detailed descriptions and illustrations are lacking, and none of Pantin's weights were signed or dated. This paperweight is one of eleven magnum-size lizard weights, each different, which are linked to Pantin through their similarities to a glass snake donated by the factory in 1880 to the Conservatoire National des Arts et Métiers, Paris.

In Egyptian myth, lizards were thought to be ethereal, flower-dwelling supernaturals. The lizards of Pantin — muscular, primal, poised at attention — are pure physicality. Like "Silkworms," the impetus behind Pantin's lizards may have been a specific event. During the 1870s, thirty dinosaur skeletons were recovered from a Belgian coal mine. This discovery could well have inspired Pantin to make its oversized, reptilian paperweights — imaginative glimpses into the Mesozoic era.

Lampwork lizard, attributed to Pantin, c. 1878 (cat. no. 56). This lizard, made in parts from color-overlaid glass rods that were reheated, fused together, and decorated with enamels, is one of eleven linked to Pantin, and the only one known to include a millefiori-cane flower. The careful rendering of the rust-red lizard and of its setting, accentuated by the striking effects of light passing through the crystal, makes this paperweight come to life in an almost eerie way.

Lampwork swan, Baccarat, c. 1850–1900 (cat. no. 33).
Enclosed in a hollow space, a white swan swims gracefully amid green plants in a small pond. Faceting complicates the views and the play of light, providing a sense of movement in this elegant piece. This type of weight was also made with two swans, a swan and two striped ducks, and three striped ducks.

Lampwork aventurine fish, Paul Ysart, c. 1969 (cat. no. 114).
Paperweight becomes fishbowl in this whimsical lampwork piece by Paul Ysart. A miniature green fish swims above a sandy ocean floor. One of the first contemporary glass artists to revive classic paperweight-making, Ysart is a third-generation glassblower.

Lampwork robin, Rick Ayotte, 1979 (cat. no. 115).
Rick Ayotte's experience as a scientific glassblower and interest
in ornithology contribute to the highly realistic depictions
of his paperweight specialty: birds in naturalistic environments.

***Lampwork and torchwork dragonfly with flowers, Orient & Flume,
1979 (cat. no. 119).*** Since 1972, when Orient & Flume
produced only surface-decorated, iridescent objects echoing the
Art Nouveau style, the studio's expertise has evolved to
include a combination of torch-applied and encased lampwork
motifs featuring a variety of flora and fauna. Millefiori
flowers, attracting a dragonfly with filigree wings, seem to come
alive in this somewhat surreal scene.

Lampwork flower, Baccarat, c. 1848–55 (cat. no. 22).
A single primrose is the focus of this Baccarat paperweight. It illustrates a relatively common practice by lampworkers: interchanging petal and leaf shapes to form various floral motifs. Baccarat mainly used just two leaf forms—oviate and lanceolate—but seldom both in one motif, as seen here.

Lampwork anemone, origin unknown, possibly Clichy, Pantin, or Bohemian, c. 1870s (cat. no. 107). Sensitively portrayed in semirelief, this anemone closely resembles its botanical likeness (blue form of the wood anemone) in J. T. deBry's *Florilegium Novum* (1612 edition). The green leaves are also botanically accurate, and the flower center comes alive with tiny beads of cobalt-blue glass.

Lampwork pansy, Val Saint-Lambert, c. 1850–1900 (cat. no. 1).
Val Saint-Lambert, founded near Liège, Belgium, in 1825,
is best known for its lead crystal, cut and engraved tablewares,
and cameo glass. A few paperweights were made there,
probably by French craftsmen, between 1850 and 1900, which
may account for the resemblance of this pansy to those
by Baccarat. However, the deep blue ground and the peripheral
pink-and-white, spiraled filigree torsade decorated with
pink and green pearls are characteristic of the Belgian glasshouse.

FLORA

While the colors and groupings of tiny, geometrically regular canes in millefiori weights give the impression of miniature gardens or bouquets, lampwork techniques allow the depiction of specific flowers. The floral motifs in French paperweights may have been selected as symbols of private sentiment or to tell the secret story of a relationship. In flower language, a gift of the ubiquitous pansy (made by all three major factories) indicated "tender thoughts" toward its recipient. A clematis expressed admiration of "mental beauty," and an anemone wistfully recalled love forsaken. Paperweight flowers were counterparts to the popular garden varieties of their time. Some were native types or ones with long histories of European cultivation. Others were relatively recent arrivals. The work of the eighteenth-century Swedish botanist Carolus Linnaeus had stimulated plant collecting and classification and encouraged scientific expeditions. Plant hunters probed mountains and jungles throughout the world in search of exotic species. Illustrated books and periodicals on the subject were hoarded by amateur horticulturists as eagerly as they were studied by designers and artists: In the last half of the nineteenth century, a profusion of flower and fruit decoration could be found in glass, jewelry, porcelain, textiles, and wallpapers.

Enthusiasm for the best botanical volumes, which blurred distinctions between art and science, was international. John James Audubon's *Birds of America*, published in London in 1827, was considered a superb flower book in itself — aside from the

Print entitled "Fritillaire Imperiale," from Pierre Joseph Redouté, *Choix des plus belles Fleurs*, Paris, C.L.F. Panckoucke (et al.), 1829. Courtesy of the Hunt Institute for Botanical Documentation, Carnegie Mellon University, Pittsburgh, Pennsylvania.

"Crown Imperial," Baccarat, c. 1848–55 (cat. no. 12).
Three crown imperial flowers are featured in this rare paper-weight. The crown imperial, a symbol of majesty, was cultivated in Persian and Turkish gardens long before its introduction to Europe. The flower appears frequently in early painting and literature. It was called the "emperor of flowers" by English dramatist George Chapman in 1595, and was mentioned by Shakespeare in *The Winter's Tale*.

birds. Among the most esteemed publications were works by Pierre Joseph Redouté (1759–1840), who for a time was supported by the patronage of Empress Josephine, painting flowers in the hothouses and gardens of her estate, Malmaison. Redouté published four books: *Les Liliacées* (1802–16), *Jardin de la Malmaison* (1803–1805), *Les Roses* (1817–24), and, finally, *Choix de plus belles Fleurs* (1827–33). Books such as these were very possibly the impetus — and perhaps even the sources — for lampwork paperweight motifs.

The crown imperial flower (*Fritillaria imperialis*), shown at left in a plate from Redouté's final book and above in a paperweight by Baccarat, was cultivated in Persia and the Near East for centuries. It was introduced to Austria in 1576, and kept in the imperial gardens in Vienna, from which it derives its European name. A legend recorded by William T. Stearn and Martyn Rix (*Redouté's Fairest Flowers* [London, 1987]) tells of this flower's presence on Golgotha during the Crucifixion: "Of all the flowers at the foot of the Cross, only the proud Crown Imperial refused to hang its head. Its flowers have hung down and wept (referring to the drop of nectar at the base of each petal) ever since."

Lampwork flower, Clichy, c. 1848–55 (cat. no. 48).
Typical of Clichy inventiveness, the extraordinary delicacy of this
pastel-toned flower, placed upon a lacy filigree ground, suggests
that it may have been made to special order for a special lady.

Lampwork fuchsia, Saint-Louis, c. 1848–55 (cat. no. 74).
The exotic fuchsia, although somewhat rare among Saint-Louis
flower paperweights, was a Victorian favorite. Its magenta
and purple colors were very much in vogue and equated with
good taste. This example, with two flowers in full bloom,
is rare. The fuchsia was named after Leonhard Fuchs
(1501–1566), a German botanist.

FILIGREE

Techniques for making the delicate, lacy patterns of filigree decoration, ancient in origin (see network bowl, p. 9) were perfected in Italy during the Renaissance and discovered about 1839 in France by Georges Bontemps, director of the Choisy-le-Roi Glassworks. By 1844, the procedure had become common knowledge at Baccarat, Clichy, and Saint-Louis. Like millefiori, filigree is a specialized cane-making process. Thin rods of opaque white glass are vertically aligned in a cylindrical mold, into which hot glass is poured. The resulting rod, now striped with white, is further encased in colorless glass, then twisted in one or more directions, and stretched to a length of twelve or more feet. When cool, the rod is cut into short segments. The ground for a pink Clichy flower (opposite, top) includes a variety of the kinds of filigree patterns that are possible using this process. Clichy and Baccarat made liberal and effective use of filigree as integral elements, accents, or grounds, for both millefiori and lampwork paperweights.

A variation of filigree in which swirls of opaque glass intersect to form a lattice-like or basket-weave pattern was used by Saint-Louis as a background for fruits and for flowers such as the fuchsia and pompon (below). New England and Boston & Sandwich also used this ground.

Like the masterful "Silkworms" (pp. 44, 48), with its radiating, white "silk," the extraordinary "Lily-of-the-Valley" illustrated on page 58 demonstrates that fili-

Lampwork pompon on vermilion-red lattice ground, Saint-Louis, c. 1848–55 (cat. no. 81). Another elaborate ground by Saint-Louis appears in this beautiful paperweight. Versatile white filigree, rare when cased with red, provides a dramatic ground for Saint-Louis's large white pompon (more often set over a transparent pink or red cushion).

The illustrations on this and the preceding page emphasize the different effects possible using a single basic technique.

"Lily-of-the-Valley," origin unknown, possibly Pantin or Bohemian, c. 1870s (cat. no. 108). Art imitates nature in this extraordinary paperweight, where the tiny blossoms of the lily-of-the-valley are realistically portrayed. The ancient art of filigree, revived as a design element for classic glass paperweights, reappears here as a gauzelike texture spread over ruby ground. The same technique was used on a blue ground for "Silkworms" (p. 48). The lily-of-the-valley traditionally symbolizes a wish for the return of happiness.

gree need not always be treated purely as background, but may also serve a thematic purpose. Both weights are unknown in origin, but they clearly seem to be related in their ingenious use of flattened filigree rods on a richly colored ground. This effect has a different feel within the separate context of each weight. Beneath a pristine spray of lily-of-the-valley, the luminous threads of filigree are suggestive of the wind-blown web of a spider.

The diminutive lily-of-the-valley is among the flowers in a bouquet (opposite) from *Collection des fleurs et des fruits* (Paris, 1805) by Jean Louis Prévost (c. 1760– c. 1810). This volume was intended to serve a variety of audiences, used as a home reference by "fathers of families" and as a source for designers of manufactured goods. The introductory text presents a history of the artistic imitation of nature beginning with ancient Greece, and, in the nineteenth-century spirit of progress, embraces the advantages of cooperation between art and industry: "Never has a century been more fertile than this in ways of using the art of imitation; and never has this art been more worthy of the great profit that the sciences, manufacturing, and commerce can draw from it."

Print from Jean Louis Prevost, *Collection de fleurs et des fruits*, Paris, 1805, with introductory
text by P. M. Gault-de-Saint-Germain, plate 2. Depicted are the lily-of-the-valley; polyanthus; deep
purple, light purple, and red anemones; red wallflower; small, double jonquil; multi-flowered
narcissus; blue hyacinth; white narcissus; double jonquil; pansy. 52.4 x 34.1 cm
The Art Institute of Chicago, gift of Mrs. W. Thorne (1940.150)

Lampwork clematis, Saint-Louis, c. 1848–55 (cat. no. 80).
A simple, ribbed, double white clematis is made
elegant in this paperweight, set on a finely spiraled blue
cushion, and seen through faceted crystal. Viewed
from above, the blossom is framed and elaborated by the
faceting of the crystal.

Lampwork pompon, Baccarat, c. 1848–55 (cat. no. 28).
A single yellow pompon flower, centered by a green-and-white
arrow cane and surrounded by a millefiori garland, is
dramatized by a star-cut base in this uncommon Baccarat paperweight. With two red buds, this example is especially rare.

Lampwork hibiscus, Clichy, c. 1848–55 (cat. no. 49).
This deceptively casual, realistic, and three-dimensional Clichy interpretation of a hibiscus flower and two buds expresses in Victorian flower language an appreciation of delicate beauty. The stems are held in a simple sheath, suggesting an impromptu token of affection.

Lampwork bouquet, Clichy, c. 1848–55 (cat. no. 47).
In soft pastel colors, three clematis-type flowers resemble the work of a master confectioner. Clichy tied the majority of its flat three-flower bouquets with ribbon (usually pink, blue, or white) and set them on colorless grounds. The double clematis-type flowers and buds are very similar, although each is paired with a different leaf form. The lettuce-green leaves closely resemble the white flower petals.

Lampwork cornucopia with bouquet, Clichy, c. 1848–55 (cat. no. 46). An uncommon Clichy bouquet is shown in a cornucopia (symbol of abundance) in this paperweight. In similar examples, a stylized head forms the closed end of the cornucopia. The buds in this painterly still life and the viola leaves in the Clichy weight below were apparently formed with identical tools.

Lampwork bouquet, Clichy, c. 1848–55 (cat. no. 51). A thought-provoking assembly of blossoms and buds by Clichy, simple at first glance, expresses unrequited love. Three types of leaves simulate those of the viola, rose, and thistle. The minute detail of buds with green sepals and stems, loosely tied with pink ribbon, make this an artful interpretation of a symbolic bouquet.

Lampwork flat bouquet, Baccarat, c. 1848–55 (cat. no. 19). In 1848, the introduction of lampwork added significantly to Baccarat's already versatile use of millefiori canes as decorative and identifying devices. Star and arrow canes center many flower types; the arrows were sometimes also used for lower pansy petals (as illustrated here) and for stylized arrangements (see below). This combination of two primroses, a pansy, and a cone rosebud is rare.

Lampwork flat bouquet, Baccarat, c. 1848–55 (cat. no. 29). The use of millefiori canes as decorative elements identify Baccarat as designer of this cruciform, flat bouquet. Typical Baccarat millefiori arrow canes form the four stylized flowers, each centered by an early Baccarat honeycomb cane. An arrow cane also centers the rare yellow pompon.

Lampwork rose, attributed to Mount Washington Glass Company, c. 1870–90 (cat. no. 92). The various manifestations of the large, beautiful American roses made by Mount Washington Glass Company reflect a knowledge of botany and express sentimental ideals: love, wedded bliss, and the utopian flower garden. In this example, note the gold ring on the hand, the butterflies with millefiori wings, and the buds in two colors, all of which combine to suggest a story of hope, love, and longing.

Lampwork flat floral spray, Baccarat, c. 1848–55 (cat. no. 23). Possibly unique, this piece displays a diminutive spray of small, lily-of-the-valley and tiny white flowers with red centers suspended over a clear, star-cut base. Viewed through one of the six side facets, the motif is further miniaturized.

A DIVERSE BOUQUET

Comparison of three paperweights, one French, circa 1848–55, one unknown in origin, circa 1848–70s, and one American, circa 1870–90, is a study in contrasts that yields a sense of the sundry decorative possibilities for glass paperweights, and of the many directions in artistic expression after 1848. At the same time, a similar concern for the symbolic meanings of the flowers they portray gives these three objects a continuity beyond their visual differences.

In terms of the floral motifs encased in paperweights, the somewhat formal compositions and stylized subjects that characterize weights of the late 1840s and 1850s — and which are exemplified by a flat, floral spray in the faceted French weight made by Baccarat (opposite, bottom) — were gradually replaced by arrangements dictated by newer tastes. There was a trend toward increasingly realistic and three-dimensional designs, as in the forget-me-nots in a basket (p. 67); at the same time, the relative restraint implied in both of these objects was abandoned by some factories for more emotional expression. Such was the case with the lampwork roses of the Mount Washington factory (see opposite, top).

Each of the three weights is enhanced, to different degrees, by faceting — reminding us that there is more to glass paperweights than the motifs encased in crystal. The angled facets and large, top window on the French weight alter its shape from spherical to nearly conical, and complicate the viewing of the flat spray of flowers within. Cutting on the bottom contributes to the elaboration of the weight's simple motif. In the case of the Mount Washington rose, however, the circular facets on the weight's side are so small as to be practically invisible from above. Rather than embellishing the lampwork motif with a forceful counterpoint, they serve as quiet foils, emphasizing by their very modesty the mass, centrality, and asymmetricality of the weight's subject. With the basket of forget-me-nots, jewel-like faceting is an integral aspect of the overall conception. In profile, the shapes and angles of the facets seem to mimic the woven contours of the basket. Viewed from above, the facets magically create a wreath from the same flowers they encircle, and provide a measured accent to the casual arrangement of the realistic flowers.

Interpreted through flower language, the three weights share a sense of longing. In its English name, the forget-me-not retains its sentimental meaning; the lily-of-the-valley, one of the blooms in the Baccarat weight, signifies a wish for the return of happiness. A longer story, but perhaps with a similar ending, is told by the American weight. Held by a right hand with a gold ring on the fourth finger, perhaps indicating lost love, a single stem unnaturally gives rise to a mature, pink rose bloom and to buds of two colors: white declares "I am worthy of you," while yellow suggests jealousy.

L UNKNOWNS

Like orphan Cinderellas, paperweights of unknown origin are sometimes among the most beautiful. The basket of forget-me-nots shown opposite, as well as the lampwork "Silkworms" (p. 48) and "Lily-of-the-Valley" (p. 58), are positive proof that unattributed weights, despite their lack of official pedigree, can exhibit exceptional artistry and workmanship.

It is possible that many such weights were made during the last quarter of the nineteenth century, after the decade-long classic period of intensive production at Baccarat, Clichy, and Saint-Louis had come to a close. The 1870s, roughly a century after the genesis of the Industrial Revolution, was a time of social and political change, and one in which all the visual arts were pulled in many different directions. In 1874, while the annual Paris Salon authoritatively exhibited works in the high tradition of French art, a diverse group of radical artists first showed their paintings together and were derisively called "Impressionists." Against the persuasive promise of more and cheaper mechanically made and ornamented goods, critics such as Englishman John Ruskin (1819–1900) championed a return to older ideals of hand-craftsmanship and simplicity in design. The glass of Emile Gallé (1846–1904), which forecast the French appetite for Art Nouveau, was said to abandon "the past for the present, the classical for the picturesque." Yet, the Venice & Murano Glass Company in Italy and Thomas Webb & Company in England maintained steady business by reviving mosaic techniques and reproducing works from Antiquity.

Following France's defeat in the Franco-Prussian War of 1871, the Paris Exposition Universelle in 1878, with the theme of "World Peace," inspired a brief resurgence of lampwork paperweights. Cristalleries de Pantin, which prepared an exhibition for that fair (see "Pantin Lizard," p. 49), has been credited with the creation of some of the most stunning, highly realistic lampwork flowers and animals. While an extraordinary but puzzling array of undocumented three-dimensional lampwork paperweights may have originated at Pantin, Bohemia is also a possible source, but, given the lack of documentary evidence, there may have been other factories about which nothing is known at present. In most cases, lost or incomplete company production records and unillustrated catalogues challenge the researcher. Thus, until new data is uncovered, the origins of these marvels of late nineteenth-century artistry remain unknown.

Lampwork forget-me-nots, origin unknown, possibly French or Bohemian, c. 1848–70s (cat. no. 105). A casual gather of forget-me-nots is preserved in a simple straw basket. The composition is elaborated by the series of windows cut on the sides and near the base, framing and miniaturizing the flowers, which are magnified only by the remaining convex surfaces of this optical masterpiece.

Profile view of lampwork forget-me-nots, origin unknown, possibly French or Bohemian, c. 1848–70s (above). The profile view of this paperweight provides an excellent sense of how faceting can transform a simple grouping of flowers into an extraordinarily complex motif.

Lampwork blue flax flower, Paul Joseph Stankard, 1978 (cat. no. 120). Paul Stankard is among the most admired of contemporary glassmakers. His blue flax flower, set against an emerald green ground, is a visual delight. The flax plant is symbolic of kindness and is cultivated for its fiber (linen) and seeds (which produce linseed oil).

Lampwork pansy, Debbie Tarsitano, c. 1978–80 (cat. no. 122). Debbie Tarsitano became interested in paperweight-making as a college student. Lampwork floral paperweights have been her full-time vocation since 1977. Her pansy, possibly inspired by a classic Baccarat prototype, is rendered in artful style and set off by a translucent cobalt-blue ground. Her *T* signature cane was changed to *DT* in 1980. Her recent work includes mixed bouquets and floral motifs combined with rural scenes engraved by former Steuben artist Max Erlacher.

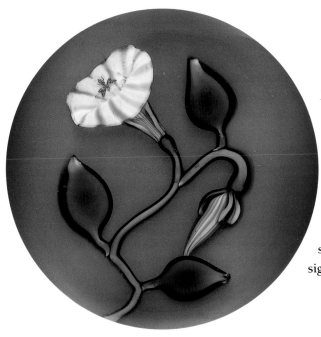

Lampwork morning glory, Charles Kaziun, 1960s (cat. no. 118).
Charles Kaziun was a pioneer of modern studio lampwork
techniques. He began his career producing ornamental glass
lampwork, and later worked in scientific glassmaking.
After seeing Evangeline Bergstrom's book *Old Glass Paperweights*
(Chicago, 1940), Kaziun was determined to revive nineteenth-
century French millefiori, silhouette, and lampwork
techniques. Shown here is an exquisite white morning glory,
striped with blue, on pink "opal" ground. Kaziun's
signature gold bee hovers over the flower.

"Braided Bouquet," Paul Joseph Stankard, 1982 (cat. no. 121).
Stankard's superlative lampwork developed from ten
years' experience in producing optical glass and complex
scientific laboratory wares. Since about 1972, paperweight-
making has been his full-time profession. Stankard's
limited-edition flowers are signed *S* near the paperweight base,
dated, and numbered. His "Braided Bouquet," signed and
dated 1982, suggests mementoes of a leisurely walk
along a country lane.

Lampwork fruit, Saint-Louis, c. 1848–55 (cat. no. 79).
Arrangements of red cherries with pears and/or apples, and leaves,
set on a double-swirl white filigree ground, were popular
Saint-Louis mid-nineteenth-century motifs (occasionally found in
doorknobs, as well). The somewhat inverted, swirled-lattice
cushion forms a funnel-shaped basket. The idea was copied by
both New England Glass Company and Boston & Sandwich.

Lampwork turnips, Saint-Louis, c. 1848–55 (cat. no. 85).
A designer's fantasy and an eye-catching interplay of colors, forms,
and textures are served up in an octafoil basket. This
Saint-Louis assembly of turnips, possibly unique, may have
been made to special order.

FRUIT

Like the decorative representations of other natural subjects in glass paperweights — flowers, plants, animals, and insects — fruit is also rich in history and symbolism. To mark civic holidays in ancient Greece, fruit was hung on temple facades between floral festoons, alternated with the skulls of sacrificial animals. This motif has continued in stone as an architectural element, and frequently appears in classically inspired ceramics, furniture, glass, and textiles of the fifteenth through eighteenth centuries. Perhaps because of their seed-bearing nature, carrying life to future generations, apples and other fruits are often associated with immortality and magic in folk legend, mythology, and proverbs. In many religions, the presentation to the deity of the first fruits of harvest represents an offering of gratitude for creation and sustenance. The excavations of the Roman cities of Herculaneum and Pompeii in the first half of the eighteenth century revealed mosaics with colorful arrangements of fruit. In a similar vein are the Dutch and Flemish still-life paintings of the seventeenth and eighteenth centuries, which celebrate fruit and vegetables of all seasons and in great variety as both signs of wealth and objects of intrinsic beauty.

Lampwork peaches, Baccarat, c. 1848–55 (cat. no. 30).
The peach, a popular French fruit of Chinese origin, has always been rich in symbolic meaning. In Victorian vernacular, peaches express that "your qualities, like your charms, are unequaled." The fruit rarely appears as a paperweight motif. Here, a simple arrangement of two peaches with green leaves is highlighted by a star-cut base.

Different symbolic interpretations of specific fruit varieties can be drawn from the classical and biblical traditions, often expressing moralistic or religious truisms. The apple, fruit of the tree of worldly knowledge in the book of Genesis, is among the oldest cultivated foods on earth. Apples were a major crop in ancient Rome, and also in Persia, where traders traveled by caravan to acquire them. They can represent temptation or the fortune of a good harvest. The cherry may indicate joy, goodness, or education, and the pear, affection. Grapes, the ancient emblem of bacchanalian revelry, also carry the Christian significance of charity, sacrifice, and redemption.

Paperweight motifs of the classic period clearly favored fruits with the most pleasant symbolism: apples, cherries, pears, and grapes (the last less common because of the complexity of depicting a cluster). The Saint-Louis turnips — not fruit but vegetables — depicted as if on a blue and white doily (p. 70, bottom), may express charity, offered with all the frills.

Lampwork and millefiori fruit and flowers, Clichy, c. 1848–55 (cat. no. 52). Fruit and flowers are combined in this Clichy weight, arranged as a central bouquet and nestled upon a white filigree ground. The elaborate, ornamental border of pastry-mold canes provides a touch of elegance. The upset filigree ground, lined with parallel white filigree rods, adds textural contrast and enhances the design. This weight compares with the New England Glass Company nosegay and pears paperweight (opposite), where the fruits seem to float in space.

Lampwork grapes, Saint-Louis, c. 1848–55 (cat. no. 71).
In addition to their metaphorical meanings, the importance of
grapes and viticulture (a French art since the sixteenth century)
make this a significant motif for a Saint-Louis paperweight.
A realistic bunch of grapes, leaves, and tiny, almost
invisible tendrils are abstracted by concave square cutting on
the dome and eight circular printies on the sides. Fine
base cutting further enhances the effect.

Lampwork nosegay and pears, probably New England
Glass Company, c. 1852–80 (cat. no. 95). The imagery created
by just one concave facet (printy) miniaturizes five
blown-glass pears and a nosegay. The combination of lampwork and millefiori canes produces a singular effect in
this paperweight — the smooth, solid forms of the lampwork
fruit contrast with the intricate, millefiori florets.

Double-swirl white filigree basket with upright bouquet, Saint-Louis, c. 1848–55 (cat. no. 72).

UNCOMMON INVENTIONS

...creative departures
   from the classic-period norm...

Discovery of the eccentric work of art is the connoisseur's delight and the epitome of collecting. Although most classic-period paperweights share a spherical shape and are intended to be viewed from above, there are many deviations from or improvisations on typical designs and techniques that spark the imagination and invite research. This chapter presents a number of rarities, specialties, and delicacies — the uncommon inventions of paperweight making. Some of these differ subtly from the classic-period norm, while others are daring departures. The reasons behind the manufacture of such uncommon paperweights can never fully be known. Whatever their origins, these weights illuminate trends in the decorative arts and fashions of their time, and provide a sense of the competitive nature of the paper-weight market, in which the rewards of novelty and refinement were financial as well as aesthetic.

By 1848, lampworking techniques, combined with millefiori elements, made possible a new array of variations, many of which catered to a taste for more realistic and three-dimensional subjects. Examples of this include Baccarat butterflies with millefiori wings and lampworked, filigree-cane bodies, and Clichy lampwork flowers within a millefiori-cane garland. The Saint-Louis basket weight shown opposite represents the achievement of a master artisan as well as displaying a refreshing awareness of the compositional potential of paperweight design. The bright, lampwork bouquet stands upright in a natural-looking basket made from double-swirl white filigree cane. The handle, a ribbon-twist rod, is held to the basket by a slice of millefiori cane on each side. The complex motif — made in separate parts and fused together — had to be reheated on a template before encasement in colorless glass by the usual paperweight-making process. The idea of encasing an upright bouquet within a basket was a fruitful one, and not exclusive to Saint-Louis, as the paperweights illustrated in the following section will demonstrate.

Concentric millefiori flowers in basket, George Bacchus & Sons, c. 1849–55 (cat. no. 6). Bacchus cog canes, in pastel colors favored by the English, are precisely arranged in a concentric pattern, simulating the most delicate of flowers at their peak. Although the canes appear to be hollow, the centers are actually transparent glass — clear and/or colored.

Profile of concentric millefiori flowers in basket, George Bacchus & Sons, c. 1849–55 (above). This view reveals the weight's shallow dome and the intricate details of the charming, white-ribbed basket with twisted rod handles.

MUSHROOMS AND PEDESTALS

There were many different approaches to the basket-of-flowers and upright-bouquet motifs. In millefiori paperweights, both looks could be abstractly expressed by drawing the canes in a tightly packed bundle down toward the base of the weight. These weights, while sometimes referred to individually as baskets, bouquets, or nosegays, have, for reasons that are visually obvious, come to be known — somewhat less poetically — as mushrooms.

Millefiori techniques were used for all the elements of the basket of flowers by the English firm of George Bacchus & Sons (p. 76). The profile view reveals a deceptively simple basket, ribbed by spaced, vertical stave rods, which supports a twisted, tricolor loop handle. Unlike the Saint-Louis basket (p. 74), the Bacchus version, which is also quite rare, lacks a high dome. The two weights share a concern for utilizing the space within the dome in such a way as to offer various viewpoints. A few handled baskets of concentric millefiori were also produced in Bohemia, but those made by Bacchus are distinguishable from them by the wonderfully loose, delicate quality of their florets. In a Bacchus variation of a formal, upright bouquet (p. 79), the traditional concentric motif arises from a white stave mushroom encircled by a

Pedestal, probably Baccarat, c. 1846–55 (cat. no. 32).
This rare Baccarat pedestal paperweight has an effect quite different from that of the Bacchus weight shown opposite. A mushroom bouquet, standing upright on a fragile stem, is encased in an elaborate yellow-and-white basket. The circular concave facets (printies) on the top and sides of this weight accentuate the delicacy of the bouquet within.

bold, red-and-white twist (torsade). Viewed from above or through the concave facets (printies), the torsade both frames the motif and interacts with it. In profile, the torsade is, by turns, intriguingly miniaturized and magnified by the cut and uncut surfaces.

The rarity of some types of basket paperweights is proof of their complexity, underscoring the problems inherent in their production. The weight illustrated on page 77 is one of only two known Baccarat examples of this type, the other with a hollow base. Horizontal rib-cutting of swirled rods in the base, and a coil of red-and-white filigree at base and rim, define the basket and add to the optic effect of printies on the top and sides. This weight, with its abstract bouquet within and an exterior, basketlike form for a base, is a most unusual glorification of the typical mushroom.

A conceptual variation of the millefiori mushroom appears in the *piedouche*, or pedestal paperweight, a form made by all of the "big three" French makers, although Clichy examples are more numerous and often more accomplished. Created from an artist's drawing dated 1848, the Saint-Louis pedestal weight on page 80 shows effective use of color-coiled filigree rods to form the pedestal. These weights are usually unfaceted, emphasizing the grandeur of the concentrically arranged florets. Clichy pedestals were also most often concentric, but are occasionally found with close millefiori or checker-pattern mushrooms with vertically striped, stave stems, on a flat, colorless foot. The illustrated example (p. 81), attractive for its pastel yellow florets and edelweiss canes, is most uncommon because of the translucence of the blue glass in its blue-and-white stave base, a colorful simulation of a basket brimming with flowers.

Concentric millefiori mushroom, George Bacchus & Sons, c. 1848–49 (cat. no. 5). Bacchus paperweights are notable for their generally pastel palette, ruffled and cog canes in concentric patterns, and large size (over 3½ inches in diameter). None were signed or dated, but in 1849 Bacchus paperweights were shown at the Exhibition of Manufactures and Arts in Birmingham, England. A strong French influence can be seen in this superb concentric millefiori mushroom.

Profile of concentric millefiori mushroom, George Bacchus & Sons, c. 1848–49 (above). The side view of this weight emphasizes the interplay of colors and visual forms achieved by faceting.

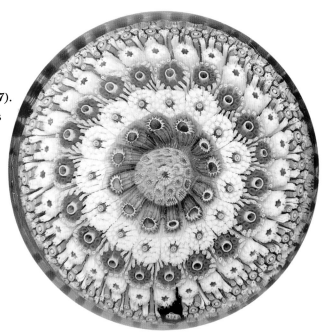

Pedestal, Saint-Louis, 1848 (cat. no. 67).
The signature and date here (*SL/1848*) make this Saint-Louis concentric millefiori pedestal especially rare. A drawing dated 1848, found in the company archives, provided the model for this Saint-Louis specialty.

Profile of pedestal, Saint-Louis, 1848 (above).
Notable is the pristine, basketlike base of double-swirl filigree with complex filigree twists encircling the rim and base.

Pedestal, Clichy, c. 1845–55 (cat. no. 53).
  This regal Clichy pedestal paperweight is remarkable for its subtle
  color scheme and use of various medallion-shaped canes.
    Almost every color available to the glassmaker was used to create
  this weight's stunning arrangement.

Profile of pedestal, Clichy, c. 1845–55 (above).
  The translucent, royal-blue stave rods used in the basket, visible
  in this view, are most unusual.

Clockwise from left: gilded lizard on blown, opaque-white base festooned with blue (marbrie), Saint-Louis, c. 1846–55 (cat. no. 64); gilded lizard on blown, blue-and-white, jasper base, Saint-Louis, c. 1848–55 (cat. no. 84); lizard on blown base overlaid with white and coral-red, cut and gilded, Saint-Louis, dated *1980* (cat. no. 113).

SPECIALTIES AND ODDITIES

While Baccarat, Clichy, and Saint-Louis each attempted very soon after 1845 to give a distinct look to their paperweight offerings, increasingly novel variations began to be manufactured by all of the major factories between 1848 and 1851. Such specialties were made available — perhaps at a surcharge — to a discriminating clientele that desired the extraordinary. Although many of these "exclusives" were produced in limited number and unsigned, they are often identifiable through their inclusion of characteristic factory canes, lampwork, colors, grounds, or other typical design components.

Saint-Louis added a fascinating new element to a few of its marbrie, jasper, and cut-overlay paperweights by crowning them with a coiled, golden lizard. These paperweights are technical, as well as aesthetic, departures from the classic-period norm: they were made by blowing glass into three-part molds and gilding the reptiles after the decorated weight had cooled. In 1980, Saint-Louis revived this form in an edition of 300 (see opposite, foreground). The deep, coral color of the overlay in the contemporary weight is unlike any used for its classic-period counterparts.

The Baccarat triple weight (p. 85) exemplifies the pride and one-upmanship that existed among the French paperweight competitors. Three paperweights in one, it naturally entailed thrice the difficulties of manufacture. Each section of this elaborate novelty includes an element that is unmistakably Baccarat: a wheatflower (top), distinctive arrow canes (center), and silhouettes on filigree (base). All three announce their Baccarat origin, as if claiming bragging rights.

Two rarities attributed to Bohemia around 1848–55 are illustrated on page 84. Both weights emphasize the prevailing vogue for floral decoration. In the first (top), compound star canes of varying heights are combined with an enameled gold-foil plaque (similar to ones sometimes used by the French) portraying a pansy and rose with green foliage. The plaque is encased above the millefiori canes, close to the weight's shallow dome. The entire surface of the other example (bottom), an encased opaque-white overlay, is hand-painted with daisies and forget-me-nots. The overall floral decoration probably relates to contemporary enamel decoration on porcelain. Traces of a gilded pattern are still visible near the base. Although it is spherical, this unsigned oddity obviously deviates from typical paperweights in which the motif is encased and magnified by a clear dome.

Millefiori with enameled foil plaque, origin unknown, possibly Bohemian, c. 1848–55 (cat. no. 103). At present, examples such as this are classified as "mystery" weights. Their canes and uneven assembly differ noticeably from those of documented French, English, or American origin. Although inconclusive, the fluorescence suggests Bohemian glass; enameled foil decoration appears in both French and Bohemian goblets, decanters, tumblers, and vases made around the years 1820 to 1860.

Painted floral, attributed to Bohemia, c. 1848–52 (cat. no. 3). In the mid-nineteenth century, an interest in botany was evident in all of the decorative arts. An unusual Bohemian paperweight, painted with a floral bouquet, thinly cased with colorless glass, and gilded, relates to the enamel decoration of porcelain and glass. Many Bohemian artisans working in porcelain manufactories painted glass tumblers and goblets in their spare time at home to sell as cabinet pieces.

Triple paperweight, Baccarat, c. 1848–55 (cat. no. 26).
This elaborate, three-in-one paperweight is an example of Baccarat one-upmanship. The vertical juxtaposition of three weights, made separately, reheated, and fused together, represents a technical achievement worth boasting about. Spaced millefiori canes in the base include deer, dog, goat, and rooster silhouettes, as well as one of a devil. In the center section, concentric circles include arrow canes. On top, a miniature weight features an upright, white-and-blue wheatflower.

Patterned millefiori double overlay, Clichy, c. 1845–55 (cat. no. 43). Most Clichy overlays are double (pink or turquoise blue over white), cut with a top printy and five side printies, with the base strawberry diamond cut. Double overlays of green, red, or dark blue over white are scarce, and white single overlays are rare. The motif is usually a concentric millefiori mushroom in a stave basket.

Mushroom double overlay, Bohemian, formerly attributed to Gilliland, c. 1848–55 (cat. no. 2). This charming paperweight is a Bohemian Biedermeier bouquet version of the French mushroom type. Placement of the windows demonstrates Bohemian faceting skills, revealing an artful creation of multiple images. The overlay paperweight technique provides an effect quite different from that of the other examples illustrated thus far. Through the use of faceting, the glassmaker carefully frames and controls each view of the central motif.

Production of a double-overlay mushroom paperweight involves several steps. First, segments of millefiori canes are arranged, in a close-pack or concentric pattern, on a collared, metal template. This arrangement, heated to about 900° F., is picked up with a gather of clear, molten glass on the end of a steel pipe, or pontil. The mushroom crown is then shaped, and a dome is formed with a second gather of glass. A "stem" is pulled from the base of the canes and enclosed in a final gather of glass. The weight, its dome still attached to the pontil, is ready for overlaying.

OVERLAYS

In paperweight hierarchy, faceted overlays, small miracles of the glassmaker's and engraver's art, rank in the upper echelon. An overlay weight is one that is covered with thin layers of one or more colors, which are cut or ground away in places to reveal the design within. Due to the technical hazards of reheating and cutting the object, successful completion of an overlay paperweight requires many skills. The colored layers must be carefully applied and the cutting must be precise to assure that the windows are uniform and the motif is centered in the weight.

Double overlay, probably Bohemian, c. 1848–55 (cat. no. 4).
In this overlay paperweight, the top printy, encircled by two rows of six side printies, creates an hexagonal form. A Bohemian version of so-called Clichy rose canes appears in one circle of this concentric pattern.

Double overlay cut with oak-leaf pattern, attributed to New England Glass Company, c. 1852–88 (cat. no. 96). A simple, spaced concentric millefiori pattern on a trellislike, double-swirl filigree ground becomes complex beneath a ruby-and-white double overlay. The overlay's motif, a hexafoil medallion surrounded by extraordinary cutting in an oak-leaf pattern, is a rare combination unknown in French paperweights.

The overlay technique requires skill and precision on the part of the glassmaker and cutter. First, an even layer of white glass is applied to the reheated weight, completely covering the sphere; then a second layer, of colored glass, is applied. To reduce glass tension and avoid cracking, the weight is annealed and slowly cooled in an oven before the exacting process of faceting begins. Any rough surfaces resulting from cutting must be polished to create fully transparent windows.

Encased double overlay with hound and stag, Saint-Louis, c. 1848–55 (cat. no. 86). When viewed from above, the exceptional bouquet within this paperweight is framed by opaque white, with three ovals cut through to clear glass in each corner of a square "mat." The process for making this rare type of paperweight required particular care to avoid cracking. First, the color-overlaid weight had to be annealed (heated and slowly cooled in an oven). After faceting was completed, the weight was reheated before being covered with a layer of molten, colorless glass.

Profile of encased double overlay with hound and stag, Saint-Louis, c. 1848–55 (above). Two of the four side facets, meticulously cut from blue to white, show animal figures. On this side is a running stag, a motif also favored by Bohemian glasshouses. The opposite side features a running hound.

Double overlay, Saint-Louis, c. 1848–55 (cat. no. 76).
Saint-Louis overlays are especially rare when not encased, as seen here. The gilt foliate decoration on the surface is an interesting finishing touch to Saint-Louis's most popular paper-weight motif, the upright bouquet. A similar example may have been exhibited in Paris in 1849.

Sulphide double overlay of Saint Louis, Saint-Louis, 1967 (cat. no. 112). In 1967, the Saint-Louis factory celebrated its bicentennial of glassmaking with a paperweight honoring Louis IX of France (1214–1270), the crusader-king who was canonized in 1297 and for whom the factory was named. This blue and white double-overlay paperweight, with a cameo of the king set in a garland of green, white, and claret-red canes, is one of a limited edition of twenty.

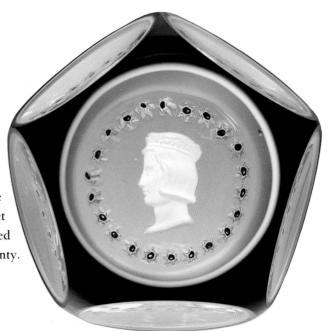

Double overlay lampwork floral, Ray Banford, c. 1984–85
(cat. no. 116). This contemporary example was probably inspired
by two unique, classic-period paperweights — the exterior
by a gingham-cut double overlay purchased by French collector
Maurice Lindon in 1978, and the interior motif by the
"Lily-of-the-Valley" in the Art Institute's Arthur Rubloff Collection
(p. 58).

Overlays epitomize the trappings of elegance sought by prospering mid-nineteenth century bourgeoisie. In Bohemia, they were sometimes shallow-cut to maximize the symmetry of the design (see p. 87). The cutting of facets not only alters the form of the weight from spherical to polygonal, but also results in multiple imagery. Large facets are referred to as windows, while smaller, usually concave ones are called printies. In a weight shown on page 86 (top), a concentric bouquet of millefiori in a stave basket receives Clichy's standard overlay treatment and is magnificent from any viewpoint. Overlays invite creative faceting, like that of six oak-leaves cut into the weight on page 88 (top), which transform the simple motif into a fascinating symbol of floriculture. Even the small areas of color that remained after faceting could be ornamented. Gilt tracery was the finishing touch added over the opaque blue of a Saint-Louis double overlay with an upright bouquet, opposite (top).

Once polished, the facets of the finished overlay paperweight become windows, revealing the motif within; in this case, a millefiori mushroom. Depending upon the number and shape of the facets, the cutter can produce a complex or simple view of the paperweight's encased imagery.

RELATED OBJECTS

The advent of millefiori paperweights in 1845 generated an array of similarly decorated objects, especially from the Saint-Louis factory. An interesting example is the handcooler, designed for use in a society that frowned upon a lady offering a warm hand to a gentleman — a sign of passion. Egg-shaped handcoolers, often faceted, make full use of the millefiori repertoire. They also may contain lampwork flowers, which are arranged singly, back-to-back, or in a dainty upright bouquet.

A natural focus of attention for a glasshouse seeking to diversify its production was the market for desk accessories, which relate to paperweights in function. Desk accessories, the tools of literacy, had evolved during the eighteenth century into emblems of the cultured life, worthy of elaborate ornamentation. In the 1770s, inkstands of gilt and painted porcelain or ceramic were the ultimate appointments for desks. The basic elements for writing — quill pen, unglazed paper, and slow-drying ink (a powder mixed with water before use) — probably made correspondence a

Clockwise from left: handcooler with animal and bird silhouettes, Baccarat, c. 1848–55 (cat. no. 27); hollow-blown handcooler with crown-type motif, Saint-Louis, c. 1848–55 (cat. no. 73); handcooler with upright floral bouquet, Saint-Louis, c. 1848–55 (cat. no. 70).

Left to right: tazza or sealing-wax-wafer stand, attributed to Saint-Louis, c. 1848–55 (cat. no. 89); pen vase, Saint-Louis, c. 1846–55 (cat. no. 13); shot vase with bell-shaped bowl, Saint-Louis, c. 1846–55 (cat. no. 62); shot vase with rib-cut, bell-shaped bowl, Saint-Louis, c. 1846–55 (cat. no. 75); stoppered scent bottle, Saint-Louis, c. 1848–55 (cat. no. 77).

frustrating exercise. Besides the inkstand, which often incorporated a candle holder and a container for sealing-wax wafers, other necessities included a razor-sharp knife for "pointing" the quill, and a pounce pot, which held gum-sandarac powder used to cover the inevitable mistakes and blotches. To assure an adequate supply of quills, prolific writers such as Thomas Jefferson raised their own geese.

The steel pen was introduced in England in 1780, but not widely adopted until after the development of mechanized papermaking, around 1809. As reading and correspondence became more common activities, penny postage was instituted in England in 1839, and postage stamps introduced in France in 1849. In the cities of England and Europe, stationery shops opened to sell writing supplies.

Saint-Louis, encouraged by its Paris retailer, Launay-Hautin et Cie., produced small vases to hold steel pens and the buckshot or sand used to keep them sharp. They also made tazzas (footed, shallow bowls) for sealing-wax wafers, and larger vases to be displayed with or without flowers on desk or mantel. All of these were set on bases resembling paperweights, and many were embellished with cutting and/or color-spiraled filigree (see above). Baccarat and Clichy also marketed desk accessories, but not in the numbers or variety of Saint-Louis. About 1848, Saint-Louis began making sealing tools with upright, lampwork bouquets encased in their handles. By that time, the desk had become as much an area for displaying these fashionable objects as for letter writing itself.

Like handcoolers and desk accessories, scent bottles were a form dear to the civilized heart. The illustrated example (above, right), with Bohemian-style cutting on white and blue overlay, is notable for its stopper, which contains an exquisite, upright bouquet.

Cameo of Queen Victoria, Baccarat, c. 1846–53 (cat. no. 8).

TO REMEMBER

...intimate keepsakes,

tributes, and souvenirs...

When it encloses an inscription or a relief image, especially the profile of a royal or sacred person, the sphere of a glass paperweight is reminiscent of the circular field of a coin or medal, objects with roots in the art and politics of Antiquity. Coins, often struck with profiles of civic deities, were both means of exchange and symbolic expressions of sovereignty as early as the sixth century B.C. The propaganda value of these small items was recognized by rulers and conquerors. The Roman emperor Hadrian (ruled 117–138) issued artistic bronze medallions, slightly larger than typical imperial coins, that carried portraits of himself and his family, along with allegorical scenes of his achievements. Hadrian's medallions were not circulated like coins, but kept or presented as gifts, to be cherished and prominently displayed. Renaissance rulers consciously revived this classical tradition, creating a vogue that survives even today. As objects primarily intended for display, paperweights are eminently suited for preserving commemorative images, and, naturally, found inspiration in the ancient custom of creating medallic memorials.

Ceramic and metallic portraits in paperweights also reflect the popularity of miniatures in the eighteenth and nineteenth centuries. Miniature portraits were painted in oils and watercolors, carved from stones and shells, cast in ceramic, glass, and metal, and cut from paper. Cameos and other miniatures were prized as intimate keepsakes or as personal expressions of tribute. The images of loved ones might be set in jewelry or carried close to the heart, while portraits of historical figures would be displayed as reminders of the virtues exemplified by the subjects' lives.

Portraiture was not the only commemorative aspect of paperweights; relief techniques were also used to depict emblems or insignia, and millefiori canes were specially made to include inscriptions or symbols. First manufactured as souvenirs of an industrial exposition in 1845, glass paperweights never fully lost their original appeal as tokens of remembrance.

Scrambled millefiori, Pietro Bigaglia, dated 1846 and 1847 (cat. no. 99). This weight commemorates the Ninth Science Congress, held in Venice in 1847. During this event, the entrepreneur Pietro Bigaglia, whose glasshouses were on the nearby island of Murano, astutely took orders for personalized paperweight souvenirs. The silhouette images of the Rialto bridge, gondola, checkerboard, and lyre, made for Bigaglia by Giovanni Battista Franchini, are all typical expressions of Venetian ambience.

"Legion of Honor" enameled foil incrustation, Baccarat, c. 1848–60 (cat. no. 31). The French Legion of Honor was originated by Napoleon as First Consul in 1802. During the Napoleonic wars, the medals were awarded to military officers and to members of the civil services. Enameled foil replicas of the medal, a symbol of French patriotism, were incrusted in goblets, tumblers, decanters, vases, and perfume bottles by both Baccarat and Saint-Louis from 1810 to 1830, and between 1848 and 1860.

"The Great Exhibition" ceramic incrustation, signed A.B. (identity unknown), Paris, c. 1851 (cat. no. 91). This artful sulphide is a souvenir of one of the Industrial Age's most important events. It commemorates the first world's fair in 1851 through a depiction of the Crystal Palace, a massive, glass structure designed specifically for the spectacle by the architect J. Paxton and built in London's Hyde Park. Most paperweights commemorating the fair include a circular sulphide medallion showing Queen Victoria and Prince Albert as well as the Crystal Palace.

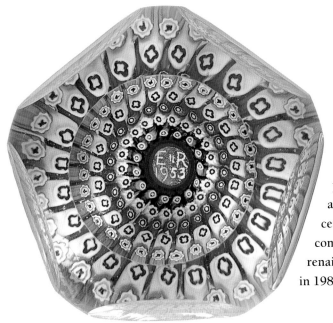

Elizabeth II coronation commemorative, Whitefriars Glass, 1953 (cat. no. 109). The center cane of this concentric millefiori paperweight, inscribed *E II R/1953*, commemorates the coronation of Her Majesty Queen Elizabeth II of England. It was produced in a limited edition of about 600 by Whitefriars Glass, a firm founded in 1680 in London on the site of a sixteenth-century monastery of the White Friars. This weight represents the company's first recorded twentieth-century, paperweight-renaissance edition. Whitefriars Glass factory closed in 1980 after years of glassmaking.

CAMEOS

Making a ceramic cameo requires a mold of the subject, which is either modeled by a skilled medalist or cast in plaster from an existing medal. The mold is then used to reproduce a bas-relief image in clay. After the clay dries, the cameo is fired in a kiln. If underfired, it is likely to crack, and overfiring causes an undesirable, glossy appearance. The finished cameo is reheated on a metal template before being encased in molten glass. Since subjects can be taken from medals, it was a relatively simple matter for independent, nineteenth-century artisans to produce cameos for sale to jewelers, glassmakers, and other craftsmen.

The casting of medals was often initiated by aristocratic or noble clients; consequently, the cameos copying these original works sometimes retain interesting political nuances. Napoleon in the guise of Caesar (opposite), perpetuated in ceramic long after his death in 1821, is a telling image of the Empire's emulation of Roman grandeur, as is the depiction of a French woman, believed to be the Empress Josephine, wearing the high-piled hairstyle of a patrician lady (opposite, bottom). The conjoined portraits of Queen Victoria and Prince Albert (below) emphasize the head that wears the crown, but also declare the unity of the royal couple. A medal marked by J. Davis, from which these profiles may have been taken, had a more specific purpose. It bears the words: *To commemorate the exhibition of all nations proposed by H.R.H. Prince Albert & patronised by H.M.G. Majesty the Queen.*

Cameo of Queen Victoria and Prince Albert, origin unknown, possibly Clichy, c. 1851 (cat. no. 100). This rare, realistically colored double portrait of Queen Victoria (1819–1901) and Prince Albert (1819–1861) may have been made for the Great Exhibition held at the Crystal Palace, London, in 1851. Prince Albert conceived of the exhibition, considered the first world's fair, as a way to advance the arts and sciences.

***Cameo of Napoleon, attributed to Clichy, c. 1846–55
(cat. no. 38).*** This ceramic portrait of Napoleon (1769–1821) was probably copied from a medal by the French engraver Bertrand Andrieu (1761–1822). In 1800, at Napoleon's direction, Andrieu began a series of medals and coins immortalizing the Emperor's career. This cameo is impressed *Andrieu* on the underside. The rough edge of the truncation — surprising in a Clichy weight — must have resulted during the firing or handling of the cameo, before it was encased in glass.

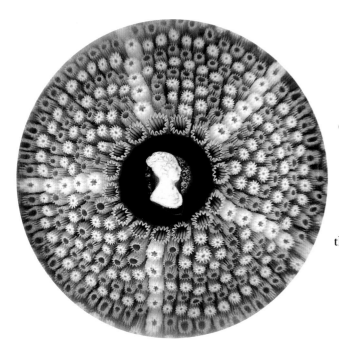

Cameo of a woman (possibly Josephine Bonaparte), Saint-Louis, c. 1846–55 (cat. no. 88). This rare, Saint-Louis patterned carpet ground is centered by a rare ceramic cameo, believed to represent the Empress Josephine (1763–1814), first wife of Napoleon I. The jewelrylike effect of this paperweight is enhanced by a carpet-ground swag surrounding the portrait.

Cameo of Benjamin Franklin, attributed to Clichy, c. 1846–55 (cat. no. 54). In 1778, when the popular American statesman, author, and scientist Benjamin Franklin (1706–1790) met his good friend Voltaire at a session of the Académie des Sciences, a contemporary source records that they "embraced amid the applause of an enthusiastic audience." The event inspired portraits of Franklin and Voltaire in almost every medium; eight different medallions copied from French terracotta and porcelain plaques were marketed by Josiah Wedgwood alone.

"Hunter and Dog" ceramic incrustation, Baccarat, c. 1846–55 (cat. no. 9). The intricacy of this detailed, traditional scene of a hunter and his dog ranks it among Baccarat's finest cameo incrustations. Set against a transparent green ground, it provides a view quite different from most of the classic-period paperweights shown thus far; here, an entire scene is depicted in a landscape setting. A similar weight, also on green ground, was given by Baccarat to the Conservatoire des Arts et Métiers, Paris, in April 1851.

Cameo of Saint Eugénie, attributed to Clichy, c. 1846–55
(cat. no. 55).   Saint Eugénie, whose legend was embellished over
the centuries, was an early Christian martyr. Her feast
day is December 25. She is shown here in a half-length portrait,
encircled by a garland of Clichy roses with edelweiss florets,
an unusual arrangement. Ceramic cameos of religious subjects were
popular adornments to tablewares and other objects made by
numerous glasshouses around 1820–40. The paperweight is enhanced
by a wide top printy and six side printies.

"Joan of Arc" ceramic incrustation, Baccarat, c. 1846–55
(cat. no. 7).   Joan of Arc (c. 1412–1431) is depicted
in a prayerful posture, holding the haft of her sword. Joan
led the troops of the dauphin Charles of France to
victory against the English in 1429. Later accused of
heresy, she was burned at the stake. A church commission
cleared her name in 1456, but she was not canonized
until the twentieth century. She is an enduring symbol of valor
and of French nationalism, which was particularly fervent
in the nineteenth century.

Pinchbeck of Leda and Jupiter, origin unknown, probably continental Europe, possibly English, c. 1848–60 (cat. no. 104). The myth of Leda and Jupiter (in the guise of a swan) is displayed in metallic relief, surrounded by a border of heart-shaped leaves.

PINCHBECKS

Pinchbeck paperweights, like cameos, utilize the properties of relief sculpture to depict detailed scenes or portraits. A pinchbeck is unlike classic paperweight types, however, in the nature of its dome and the composition of the motif it magnifies.

Pinchbeck is a metallic alloy named for its inventor, Christopher Pinchbeck (1670–1732), a London watch- and clockmaker who developed it as an imitation of gold foil for use in inexpensive jewelry. Pinchbeck jewelry was popular in Europe between 1845 and 1850. Paperweights using the alloy, while unsigned, are believed to have originated both in England and on the Continent around 1850 to 1870. In making paperweights, pinchbeck foil, eighty-three parts copper and eighteen parts zinc, was tooled over a miniature relief plaque, burnished, and sometimes hand-painted. The resulting image was then carefully lifted from its plaque and set on a marble, pewter, or wooden base, to which a hollow dome with a flat, magnifying-glass lens was screwed or cemented. The underside of the base was usually covered with leather or velvet.

Subjects were sometimes copied from famous paintings, especially landscapes or scenes of everyday life. In addition to the portrait of president Millard Fillmore and the very literal rendition of the Jupiter and Leda myth illustrated here, the Arthur Rubloff Collection includes a colored portrait of Prince Albert and a scene of feasting peasants from a painting by the Flemish artist David Teniers II.

Pinchbeck portrait of Millard Fillmore, origin unknown, English or European, c. 1850–53 (cat. no. 106). This three-dimensional portrait, skillfully painted in naturalistic colors by an unknown artist, commemorates the service of a respected American statesman, Millard Fillmore (1800–1874). Vice-president Fillmore became the thirteenth president of the United States upon the unexpected death of Zachary Taylor in 1850.

Concentric millefiori with central squirrel silhouette cane, Baccarat, 1972 (cat. no. 111)

COLLECTING

…some fragment of a dream…

The revival of paperweight-making and rejuvenation of collecting that began in 1953 with cameo incrustations by Baccarat and Saint-Louis led to Baccarat's production of patterned millefiori weights in 1957, lampwork in 1970, and, between 1971 and 1979, a collectors' series of eighteen paperweights featuring the factory's popular animal and figural silhouettes of the classic period. Inaugurating this limited edition of dated and signed concentric millefiori weights was the squirrel (opposite) in a large cane surrounded by a circle of all of the eighteen original silhouettes.

Even before the production of collectors' editions, enthusiasts sought out these glass spheres. The allure of collecting was expressed by the American writer Truman Capote (1924–1984) in the essay "The White Rose," published in his book *The Dogs Bark: Public People and Private Places* (New York, 1971). In 1947, a young, aspiring writer, Capote called upon the eminent French author Colette. Shy and nervous, he found himself gazing down at two tables laden with paperweights: "What seemed to me a magical exhibition, some fragment of a dream.... crystal spheres imprisoning green lizards,...*millefiori* bouquets, a basket of pears, butterflies alighted on a frond of fern, swirls of pink and white and blue and white, shimmering like fireworks." Colette inspired Capote to begin his own collection by giving him a Baccarat flower weight, which she called "the white rose," as a memento of his visit.

Paperweight collectors are a diverse group. Like collectors of almost anything, they tend to be true enthusiasts—not merely gatherers of objects, but people passionately interested in and drawn to the weights they collect. They can be competitive and tenacious in their quest for specific, elusive examples; many relish anecdotes about the challenges of the chase and their latest acquisitions (whether bargains or extravagances). Their motives in collecting are varied. Many paperweight collectors specialize, concentrating on paperweights with a certain motif or made by a single factory. Some collectors, for example, cultivate paperweight

Clockwise from top: burgundy-red dahlia, Baccarat, c. 1848–55 (cat. no. 20); amber-yellow dahlia, Saint-Louis, c. 1848–55 (cat. no. 82); pink-mauve dahlia, Saint-Louis, c. 1848–55 (cat. no. 69).

"gardens" limited to specific flowers, such as the primrose or the dahlia (see opposite), in all of their colors or arrangements. Such collectors may wait years before the missing pieces in their chosen specialty become available. Others may strive to assemble the best possible overview of examples from the classic period, or a representative collection of contemporary weights. In many ways, the character of a collection reflects the personality of the collector.

Like any avocation, paperweight collecting has its risks. The Baccarat pansy illustrated below, for example, is dated 1849; classic-period lampwork weights, however, were never signed or dated. The story of this spurious date begins with the hardships of World War I and the loss of the profitable Russian market after the 1918 Revolution, which put French glasshouses under great economic stress. The situation was not unlike the aftermath of the Napoleonic wars a century earlier, when hard times had motivated Saint-Louis and Baccarat to first experiment with paperweights. As part of Baccarat's modern attempts at recovery, three types of weights (garland, pansy, and sand dunes) were advertised in the 1916 catalogue. In 1925, the factory offered to add any year of the customer's choosing to a paperweight for an additional 50 centimes. While these weights are notable as bits of glass history within the context of a comprehensive collection, they do not approach the value of a true classic-period paperweight. A later Baccarat manager explained that it was assumed these dates would "fool no one, inasmuch as the appearance of the paperweights is generally mediocre." *Caveat emptor.* Let the collector beware.

Lampwork pansy, Baccarat, c. 1916–25 (cat. no. 110).
Although many paperweights can be dated and attributed according to canes included in their compositions, such documentation must be read with a degree of caution. Made for an individual order, this example bears the date *1849*; it was actually made between 1916 and 1925.

Arthur Rubloff, 1902–1983

Arthur Rubloff was born in Duluth, Minnesota, and grew up in Chisholm, on the Mesabi Iron Range. He entered the real estate business in Chicago in 1919 and started his own firm in 1929. Among the vast projects in Chicago closely identified with Rubloff are the "Magnificent Mile" of North Michigan Avenue, Carl Sandburg Village, and Evergreen Plaza shopping center, one of the first enclosed malls in the country. He was well known not only for his pioneering work as a developer but also for his charitable contributions. He donated substantially to the construction of a hospital at the University of Chicago; and buildings at the law school of Northwestern University and The Art Institute of Chicago bear his name.

Arthur Rubloff was a collector and connoisseur of many things, but first and foremost was his collection of glass paperweights. Assembled with diligence, care, and passion over twenty-five years, it remains one of the most complete collections of its kind in the world. In December 1978, Rubloff donated his magnificent collection to The Art Institute of Chicago, where a large selection of his finest acquisitions is permanently on view in the galleries of European decorative arts. Comprising 1,472 antique and modern paperweights, the Arthur Rubloff Collection remains one of the museum's most widely admired exhibits.

CATALOGUE

Listed chronologically by century, country of origin, and factory, when known. Speculative attributions to a given factory follow entries for that factory.

NINETEENTH CENTURY

BELGIUM

1. Val Saint-Lambert, Seraing, Belgium, circa 1850–1900 (p. 53)
   Lampwork pansy; two purple petals above, three rose-salmon petals below; white center cane with eight-point blue cog; white-and-pink spiral torsade on which are small "pearls," alternately green and pink; translucent, royal-blue ground; uncommon; diam. 3 in. (7.6 cm). Gift of Arthur Rubloff, 1978.1262

BOHEMIA

2. Bohemia, formerly attributed to Gilliland (American), circa 1848–55 (p. 86, bottom) Double overlay, rose-red over white; concentric mushroom formed by circles of green, red, and white millefiori canes centered by a compound cane within white stave basket; broad top printy, five almost flat side printies; star-cut base; rare; diam. 2½ in. (6.4 cm). Former collection of Col. M. Robert Guggenheim. Gift of Arthur Rubloff, 1979.820

3. Attributed to Bohemia, circa 1848–52 (p. 84, bottom)
   White overlay hand-painted with pink, yellow, and blue flowers, then thinly cased with colorless glass and further decorated with gilt vermiculation; high profile colorless base star-cut to edge; diam. 2½ in (6.4 cm). Former collection of Col. M. Robert Guggenheim. Gift of Arthur Rubloff, 1979.809

4. Attributed to Bohemia, circa 1848–55 (p. 87)
   Double overlay, red over white; spaced concentric millefiori canes include a circle of red-and-white "Clichy" roses; upset white filigree cushion; star-cut base; top printy, six circular printies above six large printies on sides; rare; diam. 2⅞ in. (7.4 cm). Former collection of Col. M. Robert Guggenheim. Gift of Arthur Rubloff, 1978.1336

ENGLAND

5. George Bacchus & Sons, Union Glass Works (Rice Harris & Company), Birmingham, England, circa 1848–49 (p. 79) Concentric millefiori mushroom; ruffled pink center cane encircled by blue, white, green, and pink cog canes and border of white and colorless rods; red-and-white torsade; top printy, six circular side printies; rare; magnum size; diam. 3⅝ in. (9.2 cm). Former collection of Col. M. Robert Guggenheim. Gift of Arthur Rubloff, 1979.846

6. George Bacchus & Sons, Union Glass Works (Rice Harris & Company), Birmingham, England, circa 1849–55 (p. 76) Basket; four concentric circles of white, blue-and-pink, pink, and white-and-blue ruffled cog canes surround cluster of seven white-and-pink cog canes centered by a blue-and-white cog cane; two twisted white loop handles striped with red and blue, one on each side of basket; uncommon; diam. 3⁹⁄₁₆ in. (9.1 cm). Gift of Arthur Rubloff, 1977.855

FRANCE

Baccarat

7. Compagnie des Cristalleries de Baccarat, France, circa 1846–55 (p. 101, bottom) Cameo incrustation; ceramic, full-length portrayal of Joan of Arc, facing right, holding a sword, her helmet and gauntlets resting on a tree stump, framed by oak and laurel branches; transparent ruby ground; top cut flat, diamond-faceted sides; diam. 3⅜ in. (8.6 cm). Bequest of Arthur Rubloff, 1988.541.635

The subject was probably taken from a marble statue of 1837 by Marie d'Orléans (1813–1839), an accomplished amateur sculptor and daughter of King Louis Philippe. The subject appeared in textile panels and other decorative items of the 1840s and 1850s. The original sculpture is in the Galerie de Louis Phillippe in the Musée de Versailles. In paperweights, the motif also appears on green, blue, and colorless grounds.

8. Compagnie des Cristalleries de Baccarat, France, circa 1846–53 (p. 94) Sulphide, incrusted ceramic cameo of Queen Victoria as a young girl, profile facing left, encircled by the words *VICTORIA I REINE DE LA GRANDE BRETAGNE*; translucent blue ground; dome cut with broad flat printy, sides diamond-faceted; diam. 3¼ in. (8.3 cm). Bequest of Arthur Rubloff, 1988.541.656

   This motif usually appears on a translucent ruby ground.

9. Compagnie des Cristalleries de Baccarat, France, circa 1846–55 (p. 100, bottom) Cameo incrustation portrays forest scene with hunter and dog on transparent green ground; wide top printy, diamond-cut sides; diam. 3⅜ in. (8.6 cm). Gift of Arthur Rubloff, 1978.1278

   A similar weight, also on green ground, was given by Baccarat to the Conservatoire des Arts et Métiers, Paris, in April, 1851: "Presse-papiers, avec camée chasse sur fond vert, lustré à facettes." The "Hunter and Dog" motif also appears on transparent red, blue, and colorless grounds.

10. Compagnie des Cristalleries de Baccarat, France, circa 1846–55 (p. 40, top) Patterned millefiori on carpet ground; six-loop garland of red, white, and blue compound canes; blue-and-white, eight-point cog canes center the six lobes, with green-and-white arrow canes between lobes; red, white, and blue arrow cane within central cluster of blue-and-white florets; white stardust-cane carpet ground; extremely rare; diam. 3 in. (7.6 cm). Bequest of Arthur Rubloff, 1988.541.239

11. Compagnie des Cristalleries de Baccarat, France, circa 1846–55 (p. 18) Patterned millefiori; double trefoil garlands of red and green canes, with yellow shamrock canes in each loop; central arrow cane within cluster of white-and-blue florets; upset white filigree ground; diam. 3¼ (8.3 cm). Bequest of Arthur Rubloff, 1988.541.261

   Although unsigned, the central arrow cane points to Baccarat as manufacturer.

12. Compagnie des Cristalleries de Baccarat, France, circa 1848–55 (p. 55) Three orange crown imperial flowers on green stalk with green leaves; extremely rare, one of three recorded examples; diam. 3 in. (7.6 cm). Former collection of Col. M. Robert Guggenheim. Bequest of Arthur Rubloff, 1988.541.272

13. Compagnie des Cristalleries de Saint-Louis, France, circa 1846–55 (p. 93, second from left) Pen vase; baluster bowl with engraved flora and vine decoration, neck and lower area cut with vertical ovals; scrambled millefiori paperweight base includes metallic green segments, ribbon twists, and blue-and-white filigree twists; height 4¹¹⁄₁₆ in. (11.9 cm), base diam. 2 in. (5.1 cm). Bequest of Arthur Rubloff, 1988.541.393

   Due to an editorial error, this Saint-Louis vase was confused with a similar Baccarat example, hence its position as no. 13 in the catalogue. This vase may have been intended to hold steel pens, but a slight residue on its interior suggests that it was used to hold fresh nosegays in water.

14. **Compagnie des Cristalleries de Baccarat, France, signed and dated** *B/1847* (p. 36, bottom) Spaced millefiori; fourteen silhouettes: two each of dog, rooster, and elephant; one each of monkey, horse, goat, squirrel, butterfly, circle of shamrocks, dove with 9 shamrocks, and dove with two shamrocks; *B/1847* signature and date cane; ground composed of segments of white filigree and yellow-and-salmon-pink ribbon twists; uncommon; magnum size; diam. 4 in. (10.2 cm). Gift of Arthur Rubloff, 1979.891

15. **Compagnie des Cristalleries de Baccarat, France, signed and dated** *B/1848* (p. 37) Close millefiori; rich variety of canes includes arrow, trefoil, shamrock, flower, and silhouettes (rooster, dog, goat, horse, deer, and white pheasant in ruby cane); base cut with wide band of cross-cut diamonds; magnum size; diam. 3⅞ in. (9.9 cm). Former collection of Col. M. Robert Guggenheim. Gift of Arthur Rubloff, 1979.918

16. **Compagnie des Cristalleries de Baccarat, France, signed and dated** *B/1848* (p. 36, top) Carpet ground; concentrically spaced arrow, geometric, and animal silhouette canes; *B/1848* signature and date cane; ground of white cog canes with blue star centers; diam. 2⅞ in. (7.4 cm). Bequest of Arthur Rubloff, 1988.541.418

    As is common in Baccarat carpet grounds, the date *B/1848* is included.

17. **Compagnie des Cristalleries de Baccarat, France, circa 1848–55** (p. 47) Lampwork flora and fauna; butterfly in profile with two mottled millefiori-cane wings and purple filigree body perched on green branch of two amethyst bellflowers; bud; foliage; top printy, six circular side printies; star-cut, colorless base; possibly unique; magnum size; diam. 3¹⁵⁄₁₆ in. (10 cm). Gift of Arthur Rubloff, 1977.845

18. **Compagnie des Cristalleries de Baccarat, France, circa 1848–55** (p. 19, bottom) Lampwork floral bouquet; four flowers: salmon-pink rose flanked by blue-and-white clematis with blue bud and yellow wheatflower with red bud, surmounted by purple-and-yellow pansy; green stems and leaves; colorless base; diam. 3³⁄₁₆ in. (8.2 cm). Gift of Arthur Rubloff, 1977.862

    This paperweight, possibly unique, is a variation of a model illustrated on a Baccarat watercolor design sheet, c. 1850.

19. **Compagnie des Cristalleries de Baccarat, France, circa 1848–55** (p. 63, top) Millefiori and lampwork; unusual dark red, cone-shaped rosebud; two primrose-type flowers (one blue and white, the other pink and white, each with stardust-cane center); early Baccarat-type pansy with rare, arrow-cane center; white bud; crossed green stems, ten green leaves; star-cut, colorless base; rare; diam. 3⅝ in. (9.2 cm). Gift of Arthur Rubloff, 1978.1251

20. **Compagnie des Cristalleries de Baccarat, France, circa 1848–55** (p. 106, top) Lampwork flower; large, burgundy-red dahlia, white stardust-cane center, small green stem, three clusters of leaves; star-cut base; extremely rare; diam. 3⅛ in. (8 cm). Gift of Arthur Rubloff, 1978.1299

    The model for this flower appears on a Baccarat watercolor design sheet, c. 1850. Baccarat's dahlia contrasts sharply with the more stylized versions by Saint-Louis.

21. **Compagnie des Cristalleries de Baccarat, France, circa 1848–55** (p. 41, top) Patterned millefiori; entwined garland forms cinquefoil, each loop consisting of different canes (yellow-and-green shamrocks, blue stardust, green, dark red, and orange); each lobe is centered by large, animal silhouette cane (horse, squirrel, deer, goat, and butterfly); cluster of white stardust canes surrounds central arrow cane; upset white filigree ground; very rare; magnum size; diam. 3¾ in. (9.6 cm). Gift of Arthur Rubloff, 1978.1347

Shamrock canes are uncommon in a garland, as is the upset white filigree ground. The central arrow cane, however, is almost a Baccarat trademark.

22. **Compagnie des Cristalleries de Baccarat, France, circa 1848–55** (p. 52, top) Lampwork flower; blue-and-white primrose, star-cane center; two types of green leaves: oviate and lanceolate; star-cut, colorless base; diam. 2¾ in. (7 cm). Gift of Arthur Rubloff, 1979.876

    This example illustrates a relatively common practice by lampworkers: interchangeable use of petal and leaf shapes to form various floral motifs. Baccarat mainly used just two leaf forms, oviate and lanceolate, but seldom both in one motif as here. A similar example, with oviate leaves only, appears on a Baccarat watercolor design sheet, c. 1850.

23. **Compagnie des Cristalleries de Baccarat, France, circa 1848–55** (p. 64, bottom) Lampwork flat floral spray; two crossed green stems: one with small, white, ribbed bellflowers, the other with tiny, red-centered, white flowers; white buds; green leaves; top printy, six side printies; star-cut, colorless base; extremely rare; diam. 2⅝ in. (6.7 cm). Gift of Arthur Rubloff, 1979.983

24. **Compagnie des Cristalleries de Baccarat, France, circa 1848–55** (p. 46, top) Lampwork flora and fauna; butterfly with mottled millefiori-cane wings, amethyst filigree body, turquoise eyes, and black antennae, above white pompon and bud; green foliage; base with wide, deep star-cutting; rare combination of butterfly and white pompon flower; diam. 3¼ in. (8.3 cm). Former collection of Paul Jokelson. Gift of Arthur Rubloff, 1979.985

    The prototype is illustrated on a Baccarat watercolor design sheet, c. 1850. Baccarat butterflies usually appear singly or within a millefiori garland on colorless or upset white filigree grounds.

25. **Compagnie des Cristalleries de Baccarat, France, circa 1848–55** (p. 19, top) Lampwork; coiled snake formed of a spiraled, green filigree rod; eyes, red mouth; sandy "rock" ground; possibly unique; diam. 3⅛ in. (8 cm). Gift of Arthur Rubloff, 1979.988

    Possibly a unique, filigree variation of the prototype shown on a Baccarat watercolor design sheet, c. 1850.

26. **Compagnie des Cristalleries de Baccarat, France, circa 1848–55** (p. 85) Triple paperweight. Base: spaced millefiori canes and silhouettes (devil, deer, dog, goat, rooster) on upset white filigree ground, diam. 2½ in. (6.4 cm); Center: three concentric circles of millefiori and arrow canes surround white stardust and red whorl floret, diameter 1¾ in. (4.5 cm); Knop: upright white wheatflower with blue dots, white whorl center, and green foliage. Diam. 1 in. (2.6 cm); rare; overall height 3½ in. (8.9 cm). Bequest of Arthur Rubloff, 1988.541.291

    A similar example is part of the Bergstrom-Mahler Museum collection, Neenah, Wisconsin; another variation is at The Corning Museum of Glass, Corning, New York.

27. **Compagnie des Cristalleries de Baccarat, France, circa 1848–55** (p. 92, background, left) Handcooler; spaced millefiori canes, animal and bird silhouettes set on upset white filigree; height 2½ in. (6.4 cm). Bequest of Arthur Rubloff, 1988.541.375

28. **Compagnie des Cristalleries de Baccarat, France, circa 1848–55** (p. 60, bottom) Lampwork flower; small yellow pompon flower centered by green-and-white arrow cane; two red buds; five green leaves; millefiori garland of alternating red and white florets; star-cut base; diam. 2⅝ in. (6.7 cm). Bequest of Arthur Rubloff, 1988.541.542

    Scarce as a Baccarat paperweight motif, the pompon was made in white, yellow, red, blue, salmon, blue-and-white, and blue/mauve/white. This example is particularly uncommon with two red buds.

29. Compagnie des Cristalleries de Baccarat, France, circa 1848–55 (p. 63, bottom) Millefiori and lampwork; cruciform flat bouquet; large yellow pompon, with green-and-white arrow cane center, flanked by alternating red and blue stylized arrow cane flowers (each centered by an early honeycomb cane); two red buds, each with green sepals; four green stems and foliage; star-cut base; rare; diam. 3⅝ in. (9.2 cm). Bequest of Arthur Rubloff, 1988.541.571

30. Compagnie des Cristalleries de Baccarat, France, circa 1848–55 (p. 71) Lampwork fruit; two peaches in naturalistic shades; branch, green foliage; star-cut, colorless base; rare; diam. 2⅞ in. (7.3 cm). Bequest of Arthur Rubloff, 1988.541.749

31. Compagnie des Cristalleries de Baccarat, France, circa 1848–60 (p. 96, bottom) Enameled silver-foil incrustation; replica of early "Legion of Honor" medal portraying Napoleon I, inscribed *BONAPARTE I, CONSUL 1802*, set on a star of five double rays over wreath of laurel and oak leaves, suspended from a red "ribbon"; garland of alternating stardust and red-and-green Baccarat arrow canes; faceted sides, star-cut base; diam. 3 in. (7.7 cm). Bequest of Arthur Rubloff, 1988.541.399

This motif was revived to commemorate the French Revolution of 1848.

Attributed to Baccarat

32. Attributed to Compagnie des Cristalleries de Baccarat, France, circa 1846–55 (p. 77) Pedestal (*piedouche*); four concentric circles of millefiori canes surround star center to form "mushroom" bouquet set on hollow, waisted, yellow-and-white basket; torsade encircles rim and foot; wide top printy, six circular side printies; one of two known, the other having a hollow base; height 3¹/₃₂ in. (7.7 cm); diam. 3¼ in. (8.3 cm). Bequest of Arthur Rubloff, 1988.541.736

A very rare Baccarat paperweight type.

33. Attributed to Compagnie des Cristalleries de Baccarat, France, circa 1850–1900 (p. 50, top) Lampwork white swan in hollow space resting on star-cut base; green- and white-speckled perimeter simulates water plants; circular printies on top and sides; extremely rare; diam. 3¼ in. (8.2 cm). Bequest of Arthur Rubloff, 1988.541.588

Clichy

34. L. J. Maës, Clichy-la-Garenne, France, circa 1845–55 (p. 20) Tricolor swirl; flat green, pink, and opaque-white rods alternately radiate from central cane of similar colors; rare; diam. 2⅝ in. (6.1 cm). Gift of Arthur Rubloff, 1977.825

Three colors in combination are found less frequently. Other combinations include blue/white/purple, green/royal blue/white, rose-pink/mauve/white, turquoise/pink/white, green/purple/white, pink/green/white, and turquoise/white/mauve.

35. L. J. Maës, Clichy-la-Garenne, France, circa 1845–55 (p. 21, bottom) Patterned millefiori; large pink-and-white "Clichy" rose encircled by two rows of large millefiori canes including yellow rose and *C* signature cane; turquoise ground lined with white; rare; diam. 2¾ in. (7 cm). Gift of Arthur Rubloff, 1978.1300

36. L. J. Maës, Clichy-la-Garenne, France, circa 1845–55 (p. 30) Patterned millefiori; closely set medallions of similar canes centered by white stardust canes; green canes with red whorls form outer circle; very rare; diam. 3³/₁₆ in. (8.2 cm). Bequest of Arthur Rubloff, 1988.541.240

37. L. J. Maës, Clichy-la-Garenne, France, circa 1845–55 (p. 31, bottom) Patterned millefiori; square design, previously unrecorded; includes row of twenty green-and-white "Clichy" roses, row of twelve pink-and-white "Clichy" roses, and one row of star canes similar to large white, red, and blue center cane; possibly unique; diam. 3 in. (7.6 cm). Bequest of Arthur Rubloff, 1988.541.262

38. L. J. Maës, Clichy-la-Garenne, France, formerly attributed to Baccarat, circa 1846–55 (p. 99, top) Cameo incrustation; ceramic cameo of Napoleon I (1769–1821), profile facing right, in guise of Roman emperor Julius Caesar (wearing laurel wreath); cameo, signed *ANDRIEU* on reverse, is set on turquoise blue ground lined with white; chip on lower right edge of cameo truncation; diam. 3 in. (7.6 cm). Bequest of Arthur Rubloff, 1988.541.794

The cloudy yellow fluorescence of this weight is closer to that of a signed Clichy weight than to that of a signed Baccarat weight, which is more peach-colored.

39. L. J. Maës, Clichy-la-Garenne, France, circa 1848–55 (p. 21, top) Lampwork bouquet; blue convolvulus (morning glory) lined with white, pink-and-white daisy, and white convolvulus edged with purple, yellow, and blue; curved green stems, two leaves; white, double-swirl filigree ground; extremely rare; diam. 2⅞ in. (7.3 cm). Bequest of Arthur Rubloff, 1988.541.343

40. L. J. Maës, Clichy-la-Garenne, France, circa 1845–55 (p. 26) Patterned millefiori; five "C" scrolls of blue, red, and white florets; edelweiss canes; pink "Clichy" roses; large white edelweiss center cane encircled by pink florets; translucent green moss cane ground with tiny white flowerheads; rare; diam. 2⅞ in. (7.3 cm). Bequest of Arthur Rubloff, 1988.541.348

41. L. J. Maës, Clichy-la-Garenne, France, circa 1845–55 (p. 32, bottom) Checker; pastry-mold canes center a checker pattern of pink, pastel green, pastel blue, and white filigree cane segments; upset white filigree ground; rare; diam. 3 in. (7.6 cm). Bequest of Arthur Rubloff, 1988.541.454

42. L. J. Maës, Clichy-la-Garenne, France, circa 1845–55 (p. 31, top) Carpet ground; carpet of white star canes with green whorl centers; numerous small millefiori canes include a "Clichy" rose and *C* signature cane; white and mauve stave rods form basket; very rare; just over miniature size; diam. 2⅛ in. (5.4 cm). Bequest of Arthur Rubloff, 1988.541.471

43. L. J. Maës, Clichy-la-Garenne, France, circa 1845–55 (p. 86, top) Patterned millefiori; double overlay, green over white; top and five side printies; concentric millefiori mushroom with green-and-pink "Clichy" rose center cane, the fourth row green-and-pink roses alternating with white edelweiss canes; white stave basket; strawberry diamond-cut base; rare overlay color; diam. 3 in. (7.6 cm). Bequest of Arthur Rubloff, 1988.541.479

44. L. J. Maës, Clichy-la-Garenne, France, circa 1845–55 (p. 41, bottom) Patterned millefiori; four intertwined quatrefoils of millefiori canes; pastry-mold and edelweiss canes surround central green floret; upset white filigree ground set on parallel rods of white filigree; diam. 3¼ in. (8.3 cm). Bequest of Arthur Rubloff, 1988.541.596

45. L. J. Maës, Clichy-la-Garenne, France, circa 1845–55 (p. 34, bottom) Swirl; dark blue and white flat rods alternately radiate from apex, surmounted by cross of various millefiori canes; rare; diam. 3³/₁₆ in. (7.9 cm). Bequest of Arthur Rubloff, 1988.541.625

The cross of millefiori canes is an unusual variation of Clichy's swirl design, which is usually centered by a single pastry-mold cane or, occasionally, a rose.

46. **L. J. Maës, Clichy-la-Garenne, France, circa 1848–55** (p. 62, top) Lampwork bouquet; ribbed pink cornucopia holds one purple and two pink dahlia-type flowers, three pink buds with green sepals, and eleven green leaves; colorless ground; very rare; diam. 2½ in. (6.4 cm). Gift of Arthur Rubloff, 1977.841

47. **L. J. Maës, Clichy-la-Garenne, France, circa 1848–55** (p. 61, bottom) Lampwork bouquet; three clematis-type flowers (pink, mauve, and white), each with two rows of veined petals, floret center; matching buds with green sepals; three different leaf forms; crossed green stems tied with blue ribbon; colorless ground; uncommon; diam. 2¾ in. (7 cm). Gift of Arthur Rubloff, 1977.844

48. **L. J. Maës, Clichy-la-Garenne, France, circa 1848–55** (p. 56, top) Lampwork flower; daisy-type flower of pink petals striped with lilac; white star-cane center outlined with burgundy; two chartreuse-yellow ribbed leaves, turquoise-green stem; ground of various types of filigree rod segments on bed of parallel white filigree rods; diam. 2¾ in. (7 cm). Bequest of Arthur Rubloff, 1988.541.491

49. **L. J. Maës, Clichy-la-Garenne, France, circa 1848–55** (p. 61, top) Lampwork flower; white hibiscus-type flower with blue shading and pink lining flanked by two partly open buds (all with green sepals), green stems in a white, blue, and pink sheath; four dark green leaves; colorless ground; exceptionally rare; diam. 2½ in. (6.4 cm). Bequest of Arthur Rubloff, 1988.541.516

50. **L. J. Maës, Clichy-la-Garenne, France, circa 1848–55** (p. 40, bottom) Patterned millefiori; double quatrefoil arrangement of white edelweiss canes and pink florets; central floret within cluster of pink-and-green "Clichy" rose canes; moss cane carpet ground with white star-cane centers; diam. 3⅜ in. (8.6 cm). Bequest of Arthur Rubloff, 1988.541.553

Although garland patterns were made by Baccarat and Saint-Louis, the great majority were made by Clichy, who produced them on clear, colored, upset filigree, and "moss" cane carpet grounds.

51. **L. J. Maës, Clichy-la-Garenne, France, circa 1848–55** (p. 62, bottom) Lampwork bouquet; viola with purple bud, pink Clichy rose with pink bud (both with green sepals), and two purple thistles with yellow centers; realistic green leaves vary with each type of flower; green stems loosely tied with pink ribbon; colorless ground; extremely rare; diam. 2⅞ in. (7.3 cm). Bequest of Arthur Rubloff, 1988.541.674

This type of bouquet is also known tied with blue ribbon on white double-swirl filigree ground.

52. **L. J. Maës, Clichy-la-Garenne, France, circa 1848–55** (p. 72) Lampwork and millefiori; two green fruit among six florets (turquoise, pastel pink, dark pink, moss green, and white), two ribbed green and pink-and-green buds surrounded by six leaves, all encircled by garland of four pink canes between each of six green-centered, purple, pastry-mold canes; upset white filigree ground on bed of parallel white filigree rods; rare; diam. 2¾ in. (7 cm). Bequest of Arthur Rubloff, 1988.541.816

53. **L. J. Maës, Clichy-la-Garenne, France, circa 1845–55** (p. 81) Pedestal (*piedouche*); concentric millefiori; central pink-and-white floret encircled by green, pink, a circle of blue-and-white and alternating pale yellow florets, green, white, and pink cog canes, a circle of alternating edelweiss and dark plum, pink, and green compound canes and alternating pink, ruby, and white canes and compound green whorls and white stars; translucent royal blue and alternating opaque white stave canes drawn toward center of colorless pedestal foot; basal ring; height 2½ in. (6.4 cm); diam. 3 in. (7.6 cm). Bequest of Arthur Rubloff, 1988.541.326

The use of translucent staves, here in royal blue, is uncommon.

Attributed to Clichy

54. **Attributed to L. J. Maës, Clichy-la-Garenne, France, circa 1845–55** (p. 100, top) Cameo incrustation; ceramic portrait of Benjamin Franklin (1706–1790), profile facing left, on colorless ground; diam. 2¹³/₃₂ in. (7.2 cm). Gift of Arthur Rubloff, 1979.772

55. **Attributed to L. J. Maës, Clichy-la-Garenne, France, circa 1845–55** (p. 101, top) Cameo incrustation; ceramic half-length portrait of Saint Eugénie, front view with head turned to left; inscribed *STE. EUGÉNIE,* surrounded by circle of edelweiss florets alternated with six pink-and-green "Clichy" rose canes; cobalt-blue ground lined with opaque white; wide top printy, six circular side printies; diam. 3¹/₁₆ in. (7.7 cm). Gift of Arthur Rubloff, 1977.834

Attributed to Pantin

56. **Attributed to Monot, Père et Fils, et Stumpf (Cristalleries de Pantin), France, circa 1878** (p. 49) Lampwork fauna; coiled, dark rust-red lizard with a line of yellow dots on its back and green, diamond markings on its sides and legs; small red-and-white millefiori-cane flower; veined, yellow-edged, long green leaves; moss-green and sand ground lined with white opaline; colorless base; high dome; one of eleven examples, each different; magnum size; diam. 4⅛ in. (10.5 cm). Gift of Arthur Rubloff, 1979.844

According to Dwight Lanmon ("A Pantin Discovery," *Paperweight Collectors' Association Annual Bulletin,* 1981; pp. 2–11, fig. 12), this is the only Pantin paperweight known to include a millefiori cane.

57. **Possibly Monot, Père et Fils, et Stumpf (Cristalleries de Pantin), circa 1878** (pp. 44, 48) Four lampwork, three-dimensional, mauve "Silkworms" on partially eaten green mulberry leaf; white filigree rods radiating like silk strands over bright, cobalt-blue ground; possibly unique; height 2¹¹/₁₆ in. (6.8 cm), diam. 3¹⁹/₃₂ in. (9.2 cm). Former collections of Mrs. Applewhaite-Abbot, Great Britain, and Paul Jokelson, New York. Bequest of Arthur Rubloff, 1988.541.195

Saint-Louis

58. **Compagnie des Cristalleries de Saint-Louis, France, circa 1845–55** (p. 33, top) Concentric millefiori; seven alternating circles of blue-and-white stars and red-and-white stars; at center, large red-and-white cog cane with central cane cluster; opaque chartreuse-yellow ground lined with white; one of two known examples; diam. 3¼ in. (8.3 cm). Former collection of Prescott N. and Sarah B. Dunbar. Gift of Arthur Rubloff, 1977.815

59. **Compagnie des Cristalleries de Saint-Louis, France, circa 1845–55** (p. 33, bottom) Patterned millefiori; alternating diamond arrangements of green and white star canes form six-pointed star centered by a pink-and-blue floret; opaque royal-blue ground lined with white; uncommon; diam. 3 in. (7.6 cm). Gift of Arthur Rubloff, 1978.1239

Typical Saint-Louis star canes also form the diamond-star garland. Saint-Louis garlands on color grounds are rare.

60. **Compagnie des Cristalleries de Saint-Louis, France, circa 1845–55** (p. 34, top) Hollow crown; alternating pink-and-green and blue-and-red ribbon twists separated by spiraled opaque-white filigree radiate from central blue cane; diam. 3¼ in. (8.3 cm). Bequest of Arthur Rubloff, 1988.541.265

61. **Compagnie des Cristalleries de Saint-Louis, France, circa 1846–55** (p. 35) Marbrie; ruby and turquoise colors festooned on opaque white sphere centered by pink, white, and blue floret; encased in colorless glass; rare with two colors; rare type; diam. 2⅞ in. (7.3 cm). Former collection of Col. M. Robert Guggenheim. Gift of Arthur Rubloff, 1979.930

62. **Compagnie des Cristalleries de Saint-Louis, France, circa 1846–55** (p. 93, third from left) Shot vase; bell-shaped bowl, blue-and-white spirals; spaced millefiori canes within garland decorate paperweight base; height 3⅝ in. (9.2 cm); diam. base 1¹³⁄₁₆ in. (4.6 cm). Bequest of Arthur Rubloff, 1988.541.386

This vase was used to hold sand or buckshot for keeping quill or steel pen points sharp. The spaced millefiori pattern in the paperweight base is uncommon.

63. **Compagnie des Cristalleries de Saint-Louis, France, circa 1846–55** (p. 22, bottom) Patterned millefiori; six slightly swirled loops of millefiori canes, centered by a compound cane, on possibly unique salmon-orange ground; diam. 3 in. (7.6 cm). Bequest of Arthur Rubloff, 1988.541.616

64. **Compagnie des Cristalleries de Saint-Louis, France, circa 1846–55** (p. 82, left) Molded, coiled lizard, gilded, on blown, opaque-white base festooned with blue (marbrie); rare type; diam. 3⅔ in. (9 cm). Bequest of Arthur Rubloff, 1988.541.820

65. **Compagnie des Cristalleries de Saint-Louis, France, signed and dated** *SL/1848* (p. 38, top) Carpet ground; rare amber-and-white cog canes with opaque-blue star centers form carpet ground that includes *SL/1848* signature and date cane; silhouettes center five spaced circles of white cog canes: dancing couple, devil, dog, and two dancing-lady silhouette canes; central compound floret encircled by eleven white cog canes; diam. 2½ in. (6.4 cm). Gift of Mrs. Potter Palmer, 1935.61

The only date used in Saint-Louis carpet ground weights was 1848.

66. **Compagnie des Cristalleries de Saint-Louis, France, signed** *SL*, **dated** *1848* (p. 22, top) Concentric millefiori; silhouettes of two dancing devils in large, white, central cog cane surrounded by five yellow matchhead canes; two circles of yellow, pink, and white canes (one with initials *SL*); circle of large silhouette canes (three camels, one bird, three dogs, and eight canes of various dancing figures); outer circle of yellow canes includes date 1848; white-lined rods form base; very rare; diam. 3 in. (7.6 cm). Gift of Arthur Rubloff, 1978.1295

Figural silhouettes, usually within a 29-point cog cane, were added to Saint-Louis millefiori motifs in 1848.

67. **Compagnie des Cristalleries de Saint-Louis, France, dated 1848** (p. 80) Pedestal (*piedouche*); six concentric circles of florets (predominantly white, blue, green, and red with pink and green centers); swirled white filigree pedestal base; red-and-white ribbon twist forms upper and lower rims; *SL/1848* signature and date cane; height 2⅝ in. (6.6 cm), diam. 3³⁄₁₆ in. (8.6 cm). Former collection of Julia S. Livengood. Bequest of Arthur Rubloff, 1988.541.328

68. **Compagnie des Cristalleries de Saint-Louis, France, circa 1848** (p. 38, bottom) Paneled jasper; alternating panels of red-and-green and blue-and-red (each with white); jasper divided into eight panels by white spokes, with a compound millefiori cane between each; central dancing-lady silhouette cane; blue-and-white torsade visible from side; diam. 3 in. (7.6 cm). Gift of Arthur Rubloff, 1979.953

69. **Compagnie des Cristalleries de Saint-Louis, France, circa 1848–55** (p. 106, left) Lampwork flower; large pink-mauve dahlia with multiple petals; green leaf tips visible at periphery; typical Saint-Louis amber-and-blue cog cane center; star-cut base; diam. 2¾ in. (7 cm). Gift of Arthur Rubloff, 1977.835

Saint-Louis adapted its double clematis to include as many as six overlapping layers of veined petals.

70. **Compagnie des Cristalleries de Saint-Louis, France, circa 1848–55** (p. 92, foreground) Handcooler; upright floral bouquet; multiple circular printies; height 2⅝ in. (6.7 cm). Gift of Arthur Rubloff, 1977.838

71. **Compagnie des Cristalleries de Saint-Louis, France, circa 1848–55** (p. 73, top) Lampwork fruit; bunch of purple grapes, brown branch, two green grape leaves, fine amber tendrils; dome cut with concave, square facets, eight circular side printies; fine strawberry diamond-cut colorless base; uncommon; diam. 3⅛ in. (8 cm). Gift of Arthur Rubloff, 1977.842

72. **Compagnie des Cristalleries de Saint-Louis, France, circa 1848–55** (p. 74) White double-swirl filigree basket contains upright bouquet of six flowerheads (pink, blue, yellow, white) with green foliage; pink-and-white ribbon twist handle, blue-and-white stardust cane terminals; very rare; diam. 3⅛ in. (8 cm). Gift of Arthur Rubloff, 1977.848

Copies of this paperweight were made in China during the 1930s.

73. **Compagnie des Cristalleries de Saint-Louis, France, circa 1848–55** (p. 92, background, right) Handcooler; hollow-blown, crown-type motif: alternating ribbon twists and filigree rods form vertically ribbed exterior; height 2¹⁵⁄₁₆ in. (7.5 cm). Gift of Arthur Rubloff, 1978.1254

74. **Compagnie des Cristalleries de Saint-Louis, France, circa 1848–55** (p. 56, bottom) Lampwork flower; two large pink-and-blue fuchsias, long stamens, three buds, and four dark green leaves on wine-red stalk; white, double-swirl filigree ground; rare with two flowers in full bloom; the ground is standard for the Saint-Louis fuchsia; diam. 3¼ in. (8.3 cm). Gift of Arthur Rubloff, 1978.1263

75. **Compagnie des Cristalleries de Saint-Louis, France, circa 1848–55** (p. 93, second from right) Shot vase; rib-cut, bell-shaped bowl, swirled blue rods and white filigree twists; rare crown-type paperweight base with alternating red and white ribbon twists and spiraled white filigree; height 3¹¹⁄₁₆ in. (9.4 cm). Bequest of Arthur Rubloff, 1988.541.317

This vase was used to hold buckshot or sand for keeping pen points sharp.

76. **Compagnie des Cristalleries de Saint-Louis, France, circa 1848–55** (p. 90, top) Double overlay; blue over white, gilt foliate decoration, contains upright bouquet of red, white, and blue lampwork flowers, two millefiori florets, and serrated green leaves; top and six side printies, base cut with deep star; extremely rare; diam. 3⅛ in. (8 cm). Bequest of Arthur Rubloff, 1988.541.371

77. **Compagnie des Cristalleries de Saint-Louis, France, circa 1848–55** (p. 93, right) Stoppered bottle; double overlay, cobalt blue over white; circular printies on shoulder, vertical faceting on sides; gilt tracery; diamond-cut stopper encloses upright bouquet; height 4¹⁵⁄₁₆ in. (12.5 cm), diam. 2⁹⁄₁₆ in. (6.5 cm). Bequest of Arthur Rubloff, 1988.541.394

78. **Compagnie des Cristalleries de Saint-Louis, France, circa 1848–55** (p. 43, top) Millefiori and lampwork; six sprigs (florets with lampwork leaf and stem) surround central sprig; one white cane with six-point star; translucent ruby base; rare; diam. 2¹³⁄₁₆ in. (7.2 cm). Bequest of Arthur Rubloff, 1988.541.398

This rare arrangement, made only by Saint-Louis, and sometimes faceted, is also known on colorless ground.

79. **Compagnie des Cristalleries de Saint-Louis, France, circa 1848–55** (p. 70, top) Lampwork fruit; apple, two pears, and four red cherries set on numerous green leaves in white, double-swirl filigree basket; diam. 2¾ in. (7 cm). Bequest of Arthur Rubloff, 1988.541.445

80. Compagnie des Cristalleries de Saint-Louis, France, circa 1848–55 (p. 60, top) Ribbed, white double clematis with opaque yellow center surrounded by pink dots, four green leaves, stem; fine, white filigree spiral on translucent blue cushion; colorless base; top printy, six side printies; diam. 3⅝ in. (9.2 cm). Bequest of Arthur Rubloff, 1988.541.498

81. Compagnie des Cristalleries de Saint-Louis, France, circa 1848–55 (p. 57) Lampwork flower; large white pompon, white bud with green sepals, green stem, four green leaves; ground of double-swirl filigree (white cased with vermilion red); rare; diam. 2¾ in. (7 cm). Bequest of Arthur Rubloff, 1988.541.574

82. Compagnie des Cristalleries de Saint-Louis, France, circa 1848–55 (pp. 23; 106, right) Lampwork flower; amber-yellow dahlia with dark-brown stripes; six emerald-green leaves and rare stem; uncommon dahlia type; diam. 2⅞ in. (7.4 cm). Bequest of Arthur Rubloff, 1988.541.580

An especially rare and dramatic Saint-Louis dahlia coloration. The multiple petals, superimposed in layers, have a three-dimensional quality. The green leaves usually appear without a stem. This stylized dahlia, composed of five overlapping layers of starflowers, is rare in amber.

83. Compagnie des Cristalleries de Saint-Louis, France, circa 1848–55 (p. 42, top) Flat bouquet; central spray of white, red, blue, and amber stylized millefiori-cane flowers; green leaves; encircled by continuous garland of similar flowers and leaves; rare; diam. 3¼ in. (8.3 cm). Bequest of Arthur Rubloff, 1988.541.590

The nosegay was produced by itself or within a circle of millefiori canes in clear glass, on upset filigree, double-swirl filigree, and on an amber-flashed base sometimes strawberry diamond cut. Saint-Louis nosegays were copied by New England Glass Company, and a few were made (usually in miniature) by Clichy.

84. Compagnie des Cristalleries de Saint-Louis, France, circa 1848–55 (p. 84, center) Molded, coiled lizard, gilded, on blown, blue-and-white jasper base; very rare on jasper; diam. 3⅜ in (8.6 cm). Bequest of Arthur Rubloff, 1988.541.627

A gilt lizard on double overlay of apple-green over white, given by Saint-Louis to the Conservatoire des Arts et Métiers, Paris, in January of 1851, is simliar to one in the Art Institute collection (no. 1979.971). It was recorded as "Presse-papiers lézard, triplé vert, taillé, huit pointils, décoré." (P. Hollister and D. P. Lanmon, *Paperweights: "Flowers which clothe the meadows."* New York: The Corning Museum of Glass, 1978.)

85. Compagnie des Cristalleries de Saint-Louis, France, circa 1848–55 (p. 70, bottom) Vegetables; five evenly spaced turnips (coral pink, lime yellow, purple, and two white) with green, leafy tops set in octafoil white filigree basket bordered in blue; extremely rare; diam. 3⅛ in. (8 cm). Former collection of Julia S. Livengood. Bequest of Arthur Rubloff, 1988.541.814

86. Compagnie des Cristalleries de Saint-Louis, France, circa 1848–55 (p. 89) Encased blue-and-white double overlay; upright bouquet centered by large pink, white, and blue-striped flower; small blue and white flowers and three millefiori cane flowers, all within swirling green leaves; two of the overlay's four side printies, cut from the blue to the white, show figures: one an opaque-white running stag and the other a running hound; star-cut base; diam. 2¼ in. (5.7 cm). Former Sinclair Collection. Bequest of Arthur Rubloff, 1988.541.819

This rare type of paperweight is usually decorated with translucent silhouettes.

87. Compagnie des Cristalleries de Saint-Louis, France, signed *SL*, circa 1845–46 (p. 29, top) Close millefiori; canes (predominantly blue, red, and white) close to glass surface; one cane inscribed *SL* in reverse; blue-and-white jasper ground; probably an early example; diam. 3⅛ in. (7.9 cm). Gift of Arthur Rubloff, 1979.906

Attributed to Saint-Louis

88. Attributed to Compagnie des Cristalleries de Saint-Louis, France, circa 1845–55 (p. 99, bottom) Cameo incrustation; ceramic portrait, profile facing right, of a woman, possibly the Empress Josephine (1763–1814), set in transparent ruby glass cane encircled by white cog canes with transparent green centers; swag carpet ground of pink-centered blue cog canes divided into five panels by spokes of pink-centered white cog canes, a circular cluster of blue, white, and orange cog canes within each panel; rare; diam. 3 in. (7.6 cm). Gift of Arthur Rubloff, 1978.1240

89. Attributed to Compagnie des Cristalleries de Saint-Louis, France, circa 1848–55 (p. 93, left) Tazza or sealing-wax-wafer stand; shallow bowl edged with pink-and-white ribbon twist; scrambled millefiori paperweight base includes white dog silhouette in ruby-and-white cog cane; height 3 in. (7.6 cm), diam. base 2⁹⁄₁₆ (6.5 cm). Bequest of Arthur Rubloff, 1988.541.387

The scrambled millefiori paperweight base is typical, but it is uncommon to find among the assortment of cane segments a white dog silhouette. Saint-Louis's multipurpose pink and white ribbon twist decorates the bowl's edge.

90. Possibly Compagnie des Cristalleries de Saint-Louis, France, circa 1848–55 (p. 46, bottom) Lampwork; millefiori-cane butterfly (uncommon in profile) hovers above bouquet of one pink and three blue primrose-type flowers; two crossed stems, seven green leaves; star-cut, colorless base; extremely rare; diam. 3⅛ in. (8 cm). Bequest of Arthur Rubloff, 1988.541.774

Butterfly motifs by Saint-Louis are extremely rare and usually appear on white, double-swirl filigree ground. In this example, the millefiori wings, body, and flowers may be unique.

French, unknown

91. Attributed to A. B. (unknown), Paris, circa 1851 (p. 97, top) Cameo incrustation; uncommon oval ceramic medallion portrays (in relief) London's Crystal Palace built in Hyde Park for the first World's Fair in 1851; inscribed in blue: *BUILDING FOR THE GREAT EXHIBITION / OF INDUSTRY OF ALL NATIONS IN LONDON 1851 / A. B. A PARIS*; diam. 2¹⁵⁄₁₆ in. (7.5 cm). Gift of Arthur Rubloff, 1979.993

UNITED STATES

92. **Attributed to Mount Washington Glass Works, New Bedford, Massachusetts, circa 1870–90 (p. 64, top)** Lampwork flower; ruffled, shaded pink, amber, and white petals with crimped edges form large rose set against four veined green leaves; green stem held by right hand wearing gold ring; five small, green leaves; yellow bud and white bud, each with green sepals; three butterflies with millefiori-cane wings hover above rose; four small circular facets on sides of weight; uncommon; magnum size; diam. 4⅝ in. (11 cm). Former collection of Old Sturbridge Village, Sturbridge, Massachusetts. Bequest of Arthur Rubloff, 1988.541.720

Paperweights were listed among Mount Washington's wares at the 1876 Centennial Exhibition in Philadelphia. A report on the event described at length Mount Washington's large crystal fountain and its "cut and molded glass, including chandeliers, busts, goblets, paperweights..." Unfortunately, the paperweights were not described. (Ingram, J. S., *The Centennial Exposition Described and Illustrated,* Philadelphia, PA: Hubbard Bros., 1876, p. 283.)

93. **New England Glass Company, East Cambridge, Massachusetts, circa 1852–88 (p. 42, bottom)** Patterned millefiori; millefiori canes set against white, double-swirl filigree ground; quatrefoil cutting (three narrow flute cuts between each lobe) on dome; four circular side printies; diam. 2½ in. (6.4 cm). Gift of Arthur Rubloff, 1979.1558

94. **New England Glass Company, East Cambridge, Massachusetts, circa 1852–88 (p. 25, left)** Fruit; blown-glass apple, shading from red to yellow and pink, speckled on one side; translucent green glass stem; flattened base; diam. 2⅞ in. (6.7 cm). Bequest of Arthur Rubloff, 1988.541.308

Blown-glass fruit was a specialty of François Pierre (1834–1872), who apprenticed at Baccarat in France before emigrating to New England in 1849. Pierre was also noted for his skills in millefiori techniques.

95. **Attributed to New England Glass Company, East Cambridge, Massachusetts, circa 1852–80 (p. 73, bottom)** Lampwork nosegay with fruit forms; three florets: pink, pastel green, and white, with cog cane centers; green stem, serrated green leaves; surrounded by five pink-and-yellow pears; top printy; colorless ground; diam. 2¹³⁄₁₆ in. (7.2 cm). Bequest of Arthur Rubloff, 1988.541.424

The fluorescence of this weight (gray) differs from that of other paperweights by both New England Glass Company and Boston & Sandwich Glass Company (bright to cloudy yellow-green).

96. **Attributed to New England Glass Company, East Cambridge, Massachusetts, circa 1852–88 (p. 88)** Double overlay, ruby over white, cut in oak leaf patterns, with hexafoil cutting on dome; spaced millefiori canes in concentric circles on swirled white filigree ground; extremely rare; diam. 2¾ in. (7 cm). Gift of Arthur Rubloff, 1979.817

97. **Attributed to New England Glass Company, East Cambridge, Massachusetts, circa 1852–88 (p. 25, right)** Lampwork flowers; three-dimensional bouquet of blue, yellow, pink, mauve, and white flowers centered by a white double clematis; white bud; green foliage; conjoined stems tied at base with a fine yellow ribbon; thin, white, double-swirl filigree ground; high dome; diamond-faceted sides; rare; diam. 3¹³⁄₁₆ in. (9.7 cm). Former collection of Julia S. Livengood. Bequest of Arthur Rubloff, 1988.541.815

This paperweight may have been made by Nicholas Lutz, who worked at New England Glass Company from 1867 to 1869. The faceting and lampwork of this superb example ranks with the best classic-period French paperweights.

VENICE

98. **Pietro Bigaglia, Venice (Murano), signed and dated *PB/1845* (p. 28)** Scrambled millefiori; includes segments of filigree twists and aventurine, four date canes inscribed *PB/1845* (three in reverse); silhouette canes: dog, three cherries, three rosebush; glittering cane in foreground is aventurine, glass in which copper particles are suspended; diam. 3³⁄₁₆ in. (8.1 cm). Bequest of Arthur Rubloff, 1988.541.285

99. **Pietro Bigaglia, Venice (Murano), signed and dated *P.B./1846* and *1847* (p. 96, top)** Scrambled millefiori canes; segments of colored rods within filigree twists; the numeral 2; *P.B. /1846* and *1847* signature and date canes; silhouettes of the Rialto bridge, cherries, a parrot, male figure, rose, crown, gondola, duck, goat, checkerboard, and lyre, interspersed with red and gold aventurine; 1847 Science Congress commemorative cane: *IX CONGRESSO DEGLI SCIENZIATI IN VENEZIA 47*; diam. 2⅛ in. (5.5 cm). Gift of Arthur Rubloff, 1979.904

ORIGIN UNKNOWN

100. **Origin unknown, possibly Clichy, circa 1845–55 (p. 98)** Cameo incrustation; rare, colored, conjoined portraits, profiles facing left, of Queen Victoria and Prince Albert; diam. 2⅝ in (6.8 cm). Gift of Arthur Rubloff, 1979.819

This weight was probably made to commemorate the Great Exhibition in London, 1851.

101. **Origin unknown, probably Bohemian (formerly attributed to Clichy), circa 1845–55 (p. 32, top)** Patterned millefiori; spaced concentric arrangement with five red-and-white "Clichy" roses, various florets, and six green-and-white "Clichy" roses; blue ground; set in blue-and-white mushroom basket encased by colorless glass; rare; diam. 3 in. (7.6 cm). Bequest of Arthur Rubloff, 1988.541.655

102. **Origin unknown, possibly Bohemian or French, circa 1846–55 (p. 29, bottom)** Mushroom; close millefiori with a predominance of blue, salmon, and green star and cross canes form mushroom encircled by unusual torsade (pink-and-white flat filigree twist coiled with blue); large, star-cut base; diam. 3⅓ in. (8.5 cm). Gift of Arthur Rubloff, 1977.811

The torsade in this paperweight was previously unrecorded. The blue coil, usually combined by Baccarat with a fine white filigree rod, here encloses a flat pink-and-white filigree twist.

103. **Origin unknown, possibly Bohemian, circa 1848–55 (p. 84, top)** Enameled gold-foil plaque (pansy, rose, green stems, and leaves) surmounts close millefiori canes, predominantly blue, and a number of six-point white star canes, all arranged in uneven heights; rare; diam. 2½ in. (6.4 cm). Gift of Arthur Rubloff, 1979.887

The canes and uneven assembly do not resemble weights signed Baccarat, Clichy, or Saint-Louis. Although inconclusive, the fluorescence (cloudy, pale yellow) suggests Bohemian glass.

104. Origin unknown, probably continental Europe, possibly England, circa 1848–60 (p. 102) Pinchbeck; Leda and the Swan within border of heart-shape leaves; lower part of medallion inscribed *JUPITER ET LEDA* and signed *THEV*; diam. 3¼ in. (8.3 cm). Bequest of Arthur Rubloff, 1988.541.419

105. Origin unknown, possibly French or Bohemian, circa 1848–70s (p. 67) Lampwork flowers; double swirl, amber-yellow filigree basket contains three-dimensional dark blue, pastel blue, pink, and white forget-me-not flowers with yellow centers and green leaves; concave top printy, two rows of circular side printies; extremely rare; diam. 3½ in. (8.9 cm). Former collection of Paul Jokelson. Gift of Arthur Rubloff, 1979.987

   Although this weight has previously been attributed to Saint-Louis, its fluorescence (cloudy, light green) is inconsistent with that of typical signed Saint-Louis weights (cloudy, coral pink).

106. Origin unknown, circa 1850–53 (p. 103)
   Pinchbeck; hand-painted, relief portrait of Millard Fillmore, front view with head turned slightly to left; name encircles portrait; thick, lenslike dome glued to metal base; diam. 3¼ in. (8.3 cm). Gift of Arthur Rubloff, 1978.1259

107. Origin unknown; possibly: L. J. Maës, Clichy; Monot, Père et Fils, et Stumpf (Cristalleries de Pantin); or Bohemian; circa 1870s (p. 52, bottom) Lampwork flower; anemone in semi-relief; ten pastel-blue, veined petals; bright yellow center with translucent, cobalt blue stamens; luxuriant green stem and large, realistic, green leaves; very rare; diam. 3 in. (7.6 cm). Former collection of Col. M. Robert Guggenheim. Gift of Arthur Rubloff, 1979.852

108. Origin unknown, possibly Monot, Père et Fils, et Stumpf (Cristalleries de Pantin), or Bohemian, circa 1870s (p. 58) Lampwork "Lily-of-the-Valley"; six white, bell-shaped flowers with yellow centers and curved green stem; surmounted by three small, white buds backed by two large, serrated green leaves; translucent red ground lined with white, overlaid with radiating white filigree; possibly unique; diam. 3⅜ in. (8.6 cm). Former collection of Julia S. Livengood. Gift of Arthur Rubloff, 1982.1480

   "Lily-of-the-Valley" appears to be related in technique and fluorescence to "Silkworms" (cat. no. 57).

TWENTIETH CENTURY

ENGLAND

109. Whitefriars Glass, Ltd., Wealdstone, England, dated 1953 (p. 97, bottom) Concentric millefiori; produced in a limited edition of about 600 to commemorate the coronation of Queen Elizabeth II in 1953; seven circles of green, white, blue, and pink canes surround central blue cane inscribed *E II R/1953*; wide top printy, five on the side; diam. 2¾ in. (7 cm). Gift of Arthur Rubloff, 1977.875

FRANCE

110. Compagnie des Cristalleries de Baccarat, France, dated 1849, circa 1916–25 (p. 107) Modern pansy, single bud, green leaves; star-cut base; made with date *1849* to customer order; diam. 2¾ in. (7 cm). Former collection of Col. M. Robert Guggenheim. Gift of Arthur Rubloff, 1979.807

111. Compagnie des Cristalleries de Baccarat, France, dated 1972 (p. 104) Concentric millefiori; central white squirrel silhouette cane encircled by blue and white florets, row of small black and white Gridel silhouette canes set in green, red florets set in yellow, and larger red florets alternated with dark and pastel blue leaves; Baccarat etched signature; diam. 3⅛ in. (8 cm). Bequest of Arthur Rubloff, 1988.541.488

   All eighteen Baccarat silhouettes of the classic period appear in this collectors' edition weight: squirrel, rooster, elephant, horse, swan, pelican, hunter, pheasant, black and white monkeys, deer, lovebirds, devil, stork, dog, goat, bird, and butterfly.

112. Compagnie des Cristalleries de Saint-Louis, France, dated 1967 (p. 90, bottom) Cameo incrustation; ceramic cameo, profile facing left, of Saint Louis (1214–1270); inscribed on the reverse *1767/SL/1967*; garland of green, white, and claret-red canes; double overlay, dark blue over white; wide top printy, five side printies; polished, flat, colorless base; limited edition of twenty; diam. 2¾ in. (7 cm). Bequest of Arthur Rubloff, 1988.541.839

   To celebrate its bicentennial in 1967, Saint-Louis created editions of twenty blue and twenty red double overlays, as well as 2,000 regular weights, with the incrusted image of the factory's patron saint.

113. Compagnie des Cristalleries de Saint-Louis, France, signed SL and dated 1980 (p. 82, bottom) Molded, coiled lizard, gilded, on blown base overlaid with white and coral-red; floral vine cutting and gilt scroll tracery; edition of 300; signed *9/300 SL*, dated *1980*; diam. 3³⁄₁₆ in. (8.1 cm). Bequest of Arthur Rubloff, 1988.541.712

SCOTLAND

114. Paul Ysart (born in Spain, 1904), Wick, Scotland, signed PY, circa 1969 (p. 50, bottom) Lampwork fauna; miniature green aventurine fish; yellow and black eyes; six bright blue spots on each side; ocean floor of rocks, shell, and "sand" highlighted with goldstone; high dome; *PY* signature cane on underside of jasper ground; polished, flat, colorless base; diam. 2¹³⁄₁₆ in. (7.2 cm). Gift of Paul Jokelson, 1973.361

UNITED STATES

115. Rick Ayotte (born 1944), Nashua, New Hampshire, dated 1979 (p. 51, top) Lampwork robin; rust-red breast, yellow beak; facing to left, perched on bare branch; colorless base engraved *Ayotte, 1979,* and 7/50; diam. 2¾ in. (7 cm). Bequest of Arthur Rubloff, 1988.541.691

116. **Ray Banford (born 1918), Hammonton, New Jersey, signed B, circa 1984–85 (p. 91)** Double overlay; dark green over white; spray of lilies-of-the-valley, green stem, and leaves on translucent, mottled, rose-red ground; signed with black B in white cane; top printy, gingham-cut sides; diam. 3 in. (7.6 cm). Bequest of Arthur Rubloff, 1988.541.850

117. **Attributed to Ralph Barber (1869–1936), Millville, New Jersey, circa 1904–1912 (p. 25, center)** Millville "crimp" rose; full-blown rose, rare in shell pink, one pink bud, with spray of green leaves; footed base; height 3⅞ in. (90.9); diam. of sphere 3½ in. (8.9 cm). Bequest of Arthur Rubloff, 1988.541.311

118. **Charles Kaziun (born 1919), Brockton, Massachusetts, signed K, circa 1960s (p. 69, top)** Lampwork white convolvulus (morning glory) striped with pastel blue; one striped blue bud with green sepals; three green leaves, stems; gold bee on inside edge of morning glory; pink opal ground lined with alabaster white; K signature cane near base; diam. 2⅜ in. (6.1 cm). Bequest of Arthur Rubloff, 1988.541.696

Kaziun's paperweights, usually less than three inches in diameter, also appear on pedestal bases and in sub-miniature size as scent-bottle stoppers. His work is identified by a fourteen-karat gold bee and/or a K cane.

119. **Orient & Flume, Chico, California, dated 1979 (p. 51, bottom)** Lampwork and torchwork; dragonfly with sky-blue body, yellow eyes, and twisted white filigree wings hovers above scattered white millefiori flowers, black and chartreuse-green fronds; chartreuse-green moss cane cushion ground; high dome; three layers; signed Orient & Flume/4 June 1979/2/50; diam. 3⅛ in. (7.9 cm). Bequest of Arthur Rubloff, 1988.541.689

120. **Paul Stankard (born 1943), Mantua, New Jersey, signed S, dated 1978 (p. 68. top)** Lampwork blue flax flower; two buds (one half open) with olive-green sepals, six olive-green leaves, stems; S signature cane at base of blue-green ground lined with white; at periphery: A/341/1978; diam. 3 in (7.6 cm). Bequest of Arthur Rubloff, 1988.541.706

121. **Paul Stankard (born 1943), Mantua, New Jersey, signed S, dated 1982 (p. 69, bottom)** Lampwork "Braided Bouquet"; pink tea rose, red bud, four white daisies (three with yellow centers, one with orange center), four yellow loosestrife (one partly open), and three blue wildflowers, one red and one yellow bud (both with green sepals; olive green stems; S cane near colorless base; marked B642/1982; diam. 3⅛ in. (7.9 cm). Bequest of Arthur Rubloff, 1988.541.847

122. **Debbie Tarsitano (born 1955), Boston, Massachusetts, signed T, circa 1978–80 (p. 68, bottom)** Lampwork pansy; upper two petals shaded blue and mauve, lower three petals rose-red striped with brown; yellow-and-black stamens; one bud at top; veined green foliage; stem; translucent dark blue ground; T signature cane on side; diam. 2⅞ in. (7.3 cm). Bequest of Arthur Rubloff, 1988.541.765

123. **Francis Dyer Whittemore (born 1921), Lansdale, Pennsylvania, circa 1960s-'70s (p. 43, bottom)** Lampwork; design low in base; two pink-and-white mistletoe bellflowers with yellow stamens; millefiori cane holding each flower, eight green leaves and stems; two bunches of white berries; translucent cobalt blue ground; W signature cane beneath one bellflower; 48 inscribed on base; diam. 2⅜ in. (6 cm). Bequest of Arthur Rubloff, 1988.541.690

Francis Dyer Whittemore spent twenty-seven years as a laboratory glassblower and color specialist. In the late 1960s, he was a lampwork consultant at the Baccarat factory.

GLOSSARY

Arrow cane. A compound glass **cane**, each component having a three-pronged, pointed arrow marking.

Aventurine. Homogeneous glass (amber, green, blue, or red) flecked with suspended copper particles.

Cane. A pencil-like glass rod with either an enclosed design running the length of the cane (visible in cross-sections), or a spiraling design on its surface.

Carpet ground. A **ground** usually composed of a single type of millefiori **cane**, producing a uniform pattern or coloration.

Close millefiori. Millefiori canes set closely together in a random arrangement (distinct from the ring patterns of **concentric millefiori**). Also called close-pack.

Checker (also _chequer_). Checkerboard pattern of canes set within squares formed by **filigree** or ribbon twist rod segments.

Cog cane. Millefiori **cane** molded to have a toothed rim, resembling the cogs on the rim of a wheel or gear.

Concentric millefiori. Circles of millefiori canes in close or spaced arrangement around a single cane or a cluster.

Crown. A paperweight, usually hollow, in which filigree rods and/or ribbon twists are vertically arranged to form a crown, with a slice of millefiori **cane** at the apex.

Cutting. A method of decorating the surface of a paperweight through the action of an abrasive wheel. Examples include flat and concave, circular or oval impressions (printies), as well as flute, star, diamond, and **strawberry-diamond** cuts. In **overlay** weights, large facets cut through one or more layers of color are called windows.

Facet. See cutting.

Filigree. A glass rod (usually colorless) with spiraled, white or colored "threads" of glass that produce the appearance of fine lace-work. A special variation that is made on a blowpipe and used as a **ground** is double-swirl filigree (also called latticinio): evenly spaced, opaque-white or colored rods embedded in colorless glass are swirled and blown into a bubble, which is then collapsed, forming a flattened, latticework ground.

Floret. A cross-section of glass **cane** with a flowerlike design.

Fluorescence. The visible radiant emission from the glass in a paperweight under long-wave ultraviolet light.

Garland. Millefiori canes arranged in single or intertwined circles, loops, trefoils, quatrefoils, etc.

Gather. Mass of molten glass held on the end of an iron or steel **pontil** rod during glassmaking. A gather of clear crystal is used to encase the decorative motif in a paperweight, forming the dome.

Ground. Background for motif: clear, colored, **carpet, double-swirl filigree, upset filigree,** etc.

Incrustation. The process of embedding a ceramic or metallic relief in glass. (See **sulphide, pinchbeck.**)

Lampwork. Technique in which an artisan uses a flame to reheat glass rods and shape them into specific objects.

Marbrie. An encased, blown, opaque-white paperweight festooned with one or two contrasting colors.

Matchhead canes. Slice of an opaque colored rod (usually sulfur yellow) used as the center of a flower.

Millefiori. Italian term meaning "thousand flowers," referring to the design in the cross-section of a composite glass **cane.**

Moss cane. A cane composed of vertical green rods (sometimes including tiny white star rods) grouped together to produce a ground resembling moss.

Mushroom. Tight arrangement of close or concentric millefiori **canes** resembling a mushroom cap, with the rods drawn down toward the base to form a "stem."

Overlay. A paperweight in which the colorless glass sphere is encased with one or more layers of colored glass, then cut through with facets to reveal the motif within.

Pastry-mold cane. Millefiori **cane** that flares out at its base.

Patterned millefiori. Millefiori **canes** arranged in definite patterns: concentric, garland, panel, spoke, star, etc., as distinguished from **close** or **scrambled millefiori.**

Pedestal. A paperweight on a basketlike pedestal or a flared foot. (French: _piedouche._)

Pinchbeck. Metallic relief made of a zinc-copper alloy, resembling gold or silver. Also, an atypical type of paperweight using this kind of relief (see p. 102).

Pontil. Long, usually solid iron or steel rod used for gathering and working molten glass and for holding a paperweight while it is being made.

Printy (also punty). Circular or oval facet. See **cutting.**

Scrambled millefiori. Haphazard arrangement of rod segments and canes. Has also been called _macédoine,_ candy, or end-of-day.

Stardust cane. Millefiori **cane** composed of very thin, white, star-shaped rods set in transparent glass, often used in clusters to form a stardust **carpet ground.**

Strawberry diamond cut. Diamond-shaped grid-cutting on the base of a paperweight.

Sulphide. A bas-relief ceramic cameo motif incrusted in paperweights and other glass objects. Also used to refer to the weights with these motifs.

Torsade. A coil or twist, colored and/or opaque white (usually enclosing a white-**filigree** core), encircling the base of a **mushroom** or upright bouquet.

Upset filigree. A **ground** composed of numerous segments of haphazardly arranged **filigree** canes, sometimes variously patterned, giving the impression of having been naturally scattered or upset by chance.

SELECT BIBLIOGRAPHY

Burke, Mrs. L.
> *The Coloured Language of Flowers.* London: Geo. Routledge & Sons, n.d.

Burton, John.
> *Glass, Philosophy and Method.* New York: Bonanza Books, 1967.

Casper, Geraldine J.
> *Glass Paperweights of the Bergstrom-Mahler Museum.* Richmond, Va.: U.S. Historical Society, 1989.

Charleston, Robert J.
> *Masterpieces of Glass: A World History from the Corning Museum of Glass.* New York: Harry N. Abrams, 1980.

Cloak, Evelyn Campbell.
> *Glass Paperweights of the Bergstrom Art Center.* New York: Crown Publishers, 1969.

Coats, Alice M.
> *The Book of Flowers.* New York: Exeter Books, 1973.

Dillon, Edward.
> *Glass.* London: Methuen, 1907.

Greenaway, Kate, illus.
> *The Illuminated Language of Flowers: Over 700 Flowers and Plants Listed Alphabetically with Their Meanings.* Text by Jean Marsh. New York: Holt, Rinehart & Winston, 1978.

Hollister, Paul.
> *Encyclopedia of Glass Paperweights.* New York: Clarkson N. Potter, 1969.

> *Glass Paperweights of the New York Historical Society.* New York: Clarkson N. Potter, 1974.

> "Muranese Millefiori Revival of the Nineteenth Century." *Corning Museum of Glass Journal of Glass Studies* volume 25 (1983): 201–206.

Hollister, Paul and Dwight P. Lanmon.
> *Paperweights: "Flowers which clothe the meadows."* New York: The Corning Museum of Glass, 1978.

Imbert, Roger, and Yolande Amic.
> *Les Presse-Papiers Français de Cristal.* Paris: Art et Industrie, 1948.

Ingold, Gerard.
> *The Art of the Paperweight: Saint Louis.* Santa Cruz, Calif.: Paperweight Press, 1981.

Jokelson, Paul.
> *Antique French Paperweights.* Privately published, 1955.

> *One Hundred of the Most Important Paperweights.* Privately published, 1966.

> *Sulphides: the Art of Cameo Incrustation.* New York: Thomas A. Nelson, 1968.

Jokelson, Paul, and Dena K. Tarshis.
> *Cameo Incrustation: The Great Sulphide Show.* Santa Cruz, Calif.: Paperweight Press, 1988.

Kulles, George N.
> *Identifying Antique Paperweights — Millefiori.* Santa Cruz, Calif.: Paperweight Press, 1985.

> *Identifying Antique Paperweights — Lampwork.* Santa Cruz, Calif.: Paperweight Press, 1987.

Kunckel, Johann.
> *Ars vitraria experimentalis oder vollkommene glasmacher Kunst.* Frankfurt and Leipzig: Verlegung Christoph Riegels, 1689.

Labino, Dominick.
> *Visual Art in Glass.* Dubuque, Iowa: Wm. C. Brown, Pubs., 1968.

McCawley, Patricia K.
> *Antique Glass Paperweights from France.* London: Spink and Son, 1968.

Manheim, Frank J.
> *A Garland of Weights.* New York: Farrar, Straus & Giroux, 1967.

Melvin, Jean Sutherland.
> *American Glass Paperweights and Their Makers.* Rev. ed. New York: Thomas Nelson, 1970.

Newell, Clarence A.
> *Old Glass Paperweights of Southern New Jersey.* Phoenix, Ariz.: Papier Presse, 1989.

Newman, Harold.
> *An Illustrated Dictionary of Glass.* London: Thames and Hudson, 1977.

Palmer, Arlene M.
> "American Heroes in Glass: The Bakewell Sulphide Portraits." *American Art Journal* XI (January 1979): 5–26.

Pellatt, Apsley.
> *Memoir on the Origin, Progress, and Improvement of Glass Manufactures: Including an Account of the Patent Crystallo Ceramie.* London: B. J. Holdsworth, 1821.

> *Curiosities of Glassmaking.* London: David Bogue, 1849.

Philippe, Joseph.
> *Le Val-Saint-Lambert.* Liège, Belgium: Librairie Halbart, 1974.

Polak, Ada.
> *Glass, Its Traditions and Its Makers.* New York: G. P. Putnam's Sons, 1975.

Rix, Martyn, and William T. Stearn.
> *Redouté's Fairest Flowers.* London: The Herbert Press, 1987.

Sarpellon, Giovanni.
> *Miniature di Vetro, 1838–1924.* Venice, Italy: Arsenale Editrice, 1990.

Selman, Lawrence H.
> *The Art of the Paperweight.* Santa Cruz, Calif.: Paperweight Press, 1988.

Whitehouse, David.
> *Glass of the Roman Empire.* New York: The Corning Museum of Glass, 1988.